PAPER
Better Design

PENCIL
Simpler Process

ERASER
Continually Improve

15 motivational life lesson stories about values clarification, goal setting and business insights to help you enjoy more success, live with significance and leave a lasting legacy

Praise for Paper Pencil Eraser

"Paper Pencil Eraser" is a self-development book that doesn't take itself too seriously, yet delivers a very serious message. The author's stories about his children and his friend Gene are particularly heartwarming. This book should appeal to anyone who seriously wants to keep their life and their family's lives moving in the right direction.

Jim Symcox
Retired Tony Robbins Coach and Copywriter, Husband and Father

"Paper Pencil Eraser" helps you take a look at your life by recognizing and understanding your true assets. William teaches us the difference between financial freedom and financial security and if you don't know the difference, this book is for you. William has a great way of detailing how you can be the author to the story of your journey through real life lessons and self-awareness by recognizing which category (whether financial or spiritual) you currently fall into and realizing which category you want to be in and explains how to get there.

Kenneth Snyder, Vice President
Sr. Commercial Real Estate Loan Officer, WaterStone Bank, S.S.B.

William has done it again by connecting simple things like manners, math skills and multi-lingual abilities to accumulating wealth. Parents and young professionals will especially resonate with the many insights contained in this book. One is how commitment is either a yes or a no, much like a pregnancy. Another is how the seven "wastes" in the production cycle can be present in our lives. If you want to improve your life, read this book, and have a pencil, paper and eraser nearby… you will understand why, very quickly.

Jonathan Dade, MBA, MTS
Author of The Church and the Community
Founder and Rabbi of Messiah Echad

Emptiness is a high state of readiness. Confused by William's quote? Then read this book for a higher level of understanding of what William is saying.

A blank sheet of paper can reveal the wisdom of a thousand words. Learn from William's take on his observations from small things in life we take for granted. How William leads his family members to greatness and won lasting friendship with his friend, Gene, is no accident. The author has a great deal of wisdom to share for all ages.

A pencil sharpened or not, in full length or half broken, can still be used to fill that blank sheet of paper with meaningful and beautiful life events. So, go ahead and dare to dream, and take an eraser along to make corrections and continuous improvements.

Juli Agustar
Founder and Executive Director, Abacus Brain Gym

"Paper Pencil Eraser" is a collection of thoughts, life stories and reflections that help the reader understand that we all have the capability to choose, determine, design, and develop our own life story. As William takes us on this journey, he also provides valuable concepts and words of advice on business and investing.

One of the ideas that stood out the most for me, both personally and financially, is that "Money you can lose and make back, but time you can only lose." This is why having a good life plan, with specific goals and a solid design, is of utmost importance.

I want to personally thank William for sharing his stories with me and for providing his guidance on becoming a better author of the book of my life. I have sharpened my pencil and accepted William's challenge to write my story. Is it time for you to sharpen your pencil and take control of your life's story?

Ana Wallace
Owner and CEO, Austin Spanish Academy

This book is a must read for any investor. William's sixth book is another powerful work of observation and reflection. It captures the essence of business thoughts and human values by using the most common objects surrounding us. He uses these to anchors guiding values. It has been a pleasure to share conversations with William as he developed the material for "Paper Pencil Eraser."

Each chapter speaks to me meaningfully, but there is one chapter that is my absolute favorite. This book has become part of my reference manual for solving problems. Each chapter stands alone and groups well into a theme, message and implementable actions.

"Paper Pencil Eraser" provides powerful, practical and simple thoughts for running my business. This book of reflections is engaging from its introduction to the simple pure message at the end. I personally used the ideas to refine my life and business purpose. Like me, you can also implement the reflections to create conversations that matter with people you care about.

James Licata
Engineer, Sailor, Investment Advisor
Westchester Equity Partners

I am glad that I got to read this book. William is undoubtedly an outstanding and inspiring storyteller. He can make readers feel tremendously engaged while reading his book. He starts with a simple thing that all of us are familiar with, and then he gradually builds deep and meaningful philosophical values out of that simple thing. Who would expect we could learn so much from an ice cream cone?

Such simple yet rich-in-context analogies are described a number of times and they make it easier for us to fully embody his concepts. I hope readers would enjoy his book as much as I did. Thank you William for sharing your wisdom with us!

Mochamad Asri
PhD candidate in Electrical and Computer Engineering
University of Texas, Austin

It takes a lot of reckoning to write a book that can help people's lives. William has written a beautiful book to help you think about what a storybook life can be. He also gives you the tools to compose one for yourself. A paper. A pencil. And an eraser.

"Paper Pencil Eraser" is the most appropriate book in an era where tsunamis of social media drown you with so much information that you are overloaded to a point where you don't know how to decide what is good for you anymore.

Being a professional architect, I understand the value of beginning with a good design on paper. This book asks and encourages you to design your life to a higher capability without losing the human side of things.

Abstract ideas are masterfully illustrated using simple everyday things we find around us. William teaches us how to use these ideas to work through challenges.

"Paper Pencil Eraser" ties in all the earlier books written by William. It is packed with logic, science, illustrations and philosophy to make the best sense of how to write your life the way you want to live. This book should be an entitlement.

Clement Teh, Architect
Owner and founder of SPACE + DIMENSIONS ARCHITECTURE

Copyright © 2019 by William Teh
ALL RIGHTS RESERVED. No part of this book may be reproduced or transmitted in any form or by any means, electronic or mechanical, including photocopying, recording or by any information storage and retrieval system, without written permission from the author, except for the inclusion of brief quotations in a review.

Publication date: March 2019
ISBN Softback: 978-0-9600503-0-7
ISBN Hardback: 978-0-9600503-1-4
ISBN eBook: 978-0-9600503-2-1
Library of Congress Control Number: 2018914486

This publication is designed to provide accurate and authoritative information in regard to the subject matter covered. It is sold with the understanding that the author or the publisher is not engaged in rendering any type of legal or professional information. If expert assistance is required, the services of a competent professional should be sought.

1. Business 2. Leadership 3. Success 4. Investing 5. Passive Income 6. Legacy 7. Goal Setting 8. Life's Lessons
I Teh, William. II PAPER PENCIL ERASER
Scripture taken from the NEW AMERICAN STANDARD BIBLE(R), Copyright (C) 1960,1962,1963,1968,1971,1972,1973,1975,1977,1995 by The Lockman Foundation. Used by permission.

PAPER PENCIL ERASER may be purchased at special quantity discounts for sales promotions, fundraising, book clubs, or educational purposes for nonprofits, schools and universities as well as rights or licensing agreements. For more information or to have William speak at your event contact him at william.teh@tttstory.com
Cover Design: David Ellsworth Information@davidellsworthdesign.com
Interior Design: Megan Van Vuren
Editors: Tracy Johnson tj@proof-your-point.com
          Mel Cohen inspiredauthorspress@gmail.com
Publishing Consultant: Mel Cohen inspiredauthorspress.com
Publisher: TTTrends Investments
Proudly Printed in the United States of America

Table of Contents

A Blank Sheet of Paper	27
Playing in the Sandbox!	33
Lessons from an Ice Cream	41
Lessons from a Beach Ball	53
Lessons from a Carton of Milk	59
Car and Driver	65
It's a Small World	79
Who is Paying for Lunch?	87
One Worm Does Not Make a Can	99
Don't Eat that Cookie	107
From Muda to Madu	121
Say the Number!	129
Full of Emptiness	141
The Last Chapter for a Good Friend	149
Composing Your Story	157

Foreword

Want to learn how to compose a better storybook life for yourself? Then this is an absolute must read book for you.

William's newest work, "Paper Pencil Eraser," continues to impress with his insightful understanding of remaining grounded in the basics. You will be amazed by what a sheet of paper, a sharpened pencil and a soft eraser can do for you. This proficiently written book is an easy fast paced read, packed with practical applications.

William's skillful reminders of proven basics with his personal examples have given us a profound and fun must read. Try to read with a highlighter in your hand to capture the many stop-and-think moments from his 15 motivational and entertaining life lesson stories.

I have read all of William's earlier books, and this one especially stands out for me both professionally and personally. William has a unique ability to gently address difficult concepts and issues using the most common everyday things we use and activities we do. He is able to delicately analyze, discuss and drive hard and difficult points home with little to no pain. Perhaps the only pain you'll feel is the blinding light of clarity after your eyes are opened.

Having personally parented an Olympic gold medalist and trained hundreds of sales professionals, I've always appreciated the necessity of teaching in simplicity. "Keep it Simple salesperson" (KISS) is a well known acronym, and I am hard pressed to find simpler tools than those found in William's new book.

On a personal note, William's chapter on emptiness and forgiveness struck a very personal chord with me. This was the most powerful chapter in the book for me. It is actually a chapter about emptiness but my focus was on something that I feel had been holding me back and that is self-forgiveness. I don't want to mess up his message but I must say thank you William for allowing me to let go of a heavy burden, move on and start with a fresh sheet of paper, pencil and softer eraser.

Michael T. Maroney

VP of Monex Deposit Company and USA Olympic Gold Medalist parent

Mike passed away on Jan. 13, 2019. The Maroney family would love everyone to remember to "pay it" forward like Mike did, whenever you get the chance. Love yourself, and be compassionate towards others. Open a door, share a smile, be your best, kindest, most courageous and giving self. Work hard, play hard, be loyal, and be faithful. Above all, trust in God, and understand the best you can, that all things in nature are perfect. It's all God's plan. God bless.

October 31, 1959 ~ January 13, 2019 (age 59)

This Book is a Gift for:

_____

Message:

_____

_____

_____

From:

_____

Acknowledgment

I am reminded that no man is an island, and there is really no such thing as a self-made man. I'd like to thank the following people, who in one way or another helped develop, contribute or support my efforts to bring this book to you.

To Dr. John Maxwell, my mentor from afar. Your values, thoughts and writings have molded much of my thinking, attitude and outlook on life.

To Mel Cohen, my editor and publishing consultant. Mel, you worked tirelessly and were always on the clock at all hours of the day and night reviewing my material and providing direction, guidance and suggestions.

To Dave Ellisworth, my cover designer for all of my books. Dave, you always took the time to listen to me. You cheerfully implemented suggestions to make the covers better.

To my wife, Sandra for helping me compose, live and polish a storybook life for our family.

To my children, Nathan and Hannah, your stories help make the book more real, down to earth, personable and fun to read.

To my friend and business partner Craig Todd. Our business experiences have helped me test some of the strategies outlined in this book. I always enjoy our business trips together, distilling our experiences into profitable strategies. You live the philosophy of friends first, business second and doing deals third.

To my friend Jim Licata. I always enjoy the pleasure of your company and growing from communicating to connecting to communion.

Dedication

To my children, Nathan (Koko Teh) and Hannah (Ah Ling), this book is dedicated to you.

My hope is to prepare you for a wonderful life ahead. Besides learning, doing and giving back which is your responsibility, my wish is to give you three magic beans called: 1) an unfair advantage; 2) a head start; and 3) a good network of people. These beans will help you to pick your way down this path called your life. You have to grow and take care of your beans in order for them to work.

The unfair advantage bean has three parts to it. They are the 3M's: Manners, Math and being Multilingual. When you have these 3M's, you can continue to accumulate the M&M's that I like.

As you know, my favorite M&M's are Money & Memories. With money, you can make good memories. With good memories, you'll want to make more money to accumulate more good memories. Remember, I think it is better to make money and earn respect.

And I believe you can have your M&M's by focusing on your big M — your Mission. When you make your mission to serve and add value to the right people, you will have overflowing abundance. More than enough to enjoy, share and spread around.

One day when Mama and I are no longer around, you can always remember your Papa in the stories I write to you, for you, and I hope will stay with you.

Papa loves you always.

Introduction

When you think about the title of this and start reading "Paper Pencil Eraser," you may think it is a book on self-help or for children ages 9 to 99. It may come across that way, but this book is probably more about my everyday observations.

I try to find lessons in ordinary simple things, like looking at a beach ball, a carton of milk, eating ice cream, or even a dirty kitchen sink.

Before we get into bouncing a beach ball or cleaning up a kitchen sink, let's consider a remarkable story about a goal-setting study carried out by the Harvard MBA program, reported by Forbes magazine.

Graduates were asked if they had set clear, written goals for their future, as well as if they had made specific plans to transform their dreams into realities.

The results of the study showed that only 3 percent of the students had written goals with plans to accomplish them, 13 percent had goals in their minds but didn't write them down, and an astonishing 84 percent had no goals whatsoever.

Consider which group you belong to. Remember, this research was conducted at the Harvard Business School, the crème de la crème of schools and graduates.

Ten years later, the same group of students was interviewed again. Here are the results:

> 13 percent of the class who had goals but did not write them down earned twice as much as the 84

percent who had no goals.

> The 3 percent who had written goals were earning about 10 times as much as the other 97 percent of the class combined.

Here's the problem with writing down goals. It seems too easy to do. Unfortunately, what is easy to do is also easy not to do. We discount the importance of writing things down on a sheet of paper. We don't believe that simply writing down our goals can have a powerful influence, impact and improve our odds of accomplishing them. In my younger days when I thought my memory was much *better*, I also incorrectly believed that success was too complicated to be simplified on a sheet of paper.

On the other hand, I believe some of us are misguided and did not learn how to write good goals. The goals we write are all about what I want or about me, Me, ME.

When we have more clarity about our purpose in life, writing and achieving our written goals should help us live our life more purposefully, intentionally and steadfastly. Goals serve as good milestones to living our lives more purposefully.

Breaking it down

Living a better life can be simpler if we are able to break it down into three simple-to-understand components like a piece of Paper, a Pencil and an Eraser.

Paper

The chapters with a Paper heading are about designing a better life. We can draft, draw or doodle our design on paper.

Thinking for most people seems to be a difficult activity. Maybe that's why so few people do it.

Reflecting on my engineering days, I learned that reliability is a byproduct of design.

If we start off with a poor design—no matter how hard we work—we will always struggle. It is like choosing to ride a bicycle to race against someone on a motorcycle. In the long run, we can't win with working harder against someone that is working smarter by using a better design.

When we can think it right, it is much easier to do it right. It's better to work on doing the right things poorly at first and get better at them over time, than doing the wrong things well.

We will regret the time we lose or misuse to discover that we were working on the wrong things. What's worse is waking up one day and discovering we don't have the time, energy and right skills sets to recover and start over again. We can't turn back the hands of time.

Pencil

The chapters with a Pencil heading are about the process, or doing. Again, back in my engineering days, I learned that quality is a byproduct of process control.

The better we can control our process, the more consistently we can deliver our product or service.

The simpler the process, the more transparent work becomes. It is easier and quicker to pick out where mistakes are made. A good process should also be repeatable.

Being different doesn't matter if you're useless.

Sometimes people try to do it their way just for the sake of being different; or they are just not willing to follow a proven formula or process. Doing things differently just to be different doesn't matter if we can't get the desired results.

Worse yet is not knowing what results you want to get by being different.

These rebels may sometimes just not have a good cause and create more problems than good.

Five Lessons we can learn from a pencil:

1. Everything you do will leave a mark.

2. What's important is inside of you, not outside.

3. You will undergo painful sharpening that will make you better. You will also get shorter. That is the price of experience.

4. To be the best you can be, you should allow yourself to be guided by the hand that holds you. So pick a good hand.

5. We used pencils when we were young, but now we write with pens. Why? Because mistakes in childhood can be more easily erased — but not later in adulthood.

Eraser

The chapters with an Eraser heading talk about correcting, cleaning, cleansing and continually improving.

Five Lessons we can learn from an eraser:

1. If you can't be a pencil to write someone's happiness, then try to be a caring eraser to remove their sadness.
2. You will make mistakes. That's why pencils have erasers.
3. You can use an eraser on the drafting table or a sledgehammer on the construction site.
4. No matter how hard you erase, you will always leave a mark.
5. Pencils come with erasers. Pens don't.

For those of us trying to live better or better our lives, I believe we should invest at least two-thirds of our effort to designing, redesigning or starting a completely new design for our life, and one-third working on the process. Remember the race between the bicycle and the motorcycle?

Progressing from struggling to surviving to succeeding can take less effort if we work off a better design. Consider chopping wood with an axe, then chopping wood with a power chainsaw, then hiring a crew to chop the wood for you. We can actually accomplish more by doing less. It is all about the design. We can own the design and delegate the process for success.

When we start thinking about our life as a business, we can design a better business and life. So what is a business? I believe any time we have to make a choice it is a business.

Do think through my thoughts about using a paper, pencil and eraser to capture, compose and live a storybook life.

In my storybook of life, I have many eraser marks. I have even torn or made holes in the paper where I have tried to rub out some bad pencil or rather pen marks I wished I had not made.

I do not regret making mistakes that cost me time and money when I was able to learn from them and did not repeat them. If I knew how to ask for the right help, I could have made my mistakes earlier, smaller and quicker. This would have let me to move on faster, or lose less money.

But I do regret the grievances I held on to longer than I should have. I do regret the harsh words I carelessly said that hurt someone, especially those near and dear to me. I do regret the inconsiderate and unkind acts I did, especially those times where I was not aware of the negative impact of my actions. I especially regret all the relationships I harmed and did not mend because of my inflated ego or pride.

I believe regret is part of learning. Used properly, regret can help internalize what we learned from our mess ups and anchor the lessons learned from our mistakes. I hear so many people proudly say they have made mistakes but have no regrets. I find that very hard to believe. Perhaps it is a way of not acknowledging fault or protecting their feelings. Without regret, there can be no real healing for a hurt we caused to another or to ourselves.

I hope my stories can touch your heart, perhaps change your mind, and hopefully hold your hand to sidestep some of the mistakes I have made.

I look forward to visiting with you again at the back of the book.

Chapter 1

A Blank Sheet of Paper

"Fill your paper with the breathings of your heart."
—William Wordsworth

According to the United Nations, there were 7.6 billion people in the world in June 2017.

Of the over 7 billion people on earth, what percent of people do you think know their purpose with crystal clear clarity and are living a life that is a true and authentic reflection of their purpose?

The answer may shock, surprise or stun you. Numerous studies have shown that only about 3 percent of the population set goals, and only about 1 percent actually write them down.

So would it be safe to say that over 95 percent of us simply drift through life?

Human beings are quite a remarkable species. No other species, plants or animals live their lives less than they are capable of doing. What is it that makes people live less or below than they are capable of doing or being? Could it be a sense of security? In prison, there is a term called *maximum security*; this represents the most secure levels of custody. I have also heard maximum security called minimum freedom. Some people trade freedom for security.

Wild animals kept in captivity that have security, but no freedom, eventually lose their drive to live. Even worse, they can become crazy (e.g., killer whales in captivity). Did you know that killer whales are stressed out living in giant fish tanks? ALL captive male killer whales have a collapsed dorsal fin. Killer whales are not designed to live in a big fish bowl. They have no place to swim freely, and they eat an unnatural diet of thawed dead fish.

> *"Forced security kills the spirit."*
> —William Teh

Besides humans, I don't know of any other living creature that has a *CHOICE* to design, develop and determine how they'd like to live their lives.

A design is usually born on paper.

Take the bridge, boat or plane builder for example. There are basic laws of physics and good design practices that have been time tested, proven out, and must be followed.

A bridge is designed and built to be able to carry the weight. A boat is designed and built to float. A plane is designed and built to take off, fly and land. If the engineer does not obey the laws of gravity and physics, bridges will break, boats will sink, and planes will crash.

Here is where the professionals differ from the amateurs. They understand that it is not necessary to repeat the learning experiences of those who have done it before them. They can improve on what has already been tested, proven and works.

I would argue that, at least 95 percent of the time, designers and builders follow a proven template for their creations.

What is a template? A template is a form or pattern used as a guide to make something. Using a template correctly can save us time, energy and pain from repeating past mistakes, while leveraging the lessons of what worked and still works.

What do you think is the MOST important project that we can design and build for ourselves? Perhaps — our LIFE?

The Oxford English Dictionary contains 171,476 words. Of the 170 thousand-plus words, an average native English speaker uses about 5,000 words in their speech and about 10,000 words in their writing (https://www.bellenglish.com Learning Resources, Ken Bateup, 1 June 2016).

If I understand this correctly, we barely use less than 6 percent of the words in the English language to communicate. And for most of us, we are satisfied or not dissatisfied with that level of mastery.

So I think for about 95 percent of us, 95 percent of the things we want to accomplish and do already has a template out there that we can use.

For the other 5 percent of us, the 5 percent of things we want to accomplish will probably require us to start with a blank sheet of paper. I will leave that up to the future Einstein's, Newton's and Da Vinci's.

Public media has been feeding us so much bad information. Worse yet, we can't tell what is good from the bad and we actually believe what we hear and see with little questioning. We read propaganda such as, "Go where no man has gone before." "Be the first." "Make your own path." "Be an army of one." On and on.

> *"Sometimes the road less travelled is less travelled for a reason."*
>
> —*Jerry Seinfeld*

Perhaps we should interview the other 99 out of 100 people that failed, crashed and never recovered from believing and acting on popular propaganda.

American born author, entrepreneur and life coach Tony Robbins says, "Success leaves clues. Go figure out what someone who was successful did, model it, improve it and learn their steps. They have knowledge." Sounds like a success template to me.

I believe approximately 95 percent of us do not think about designing or building a better life; we just *wing it* and live it day by day and hope that things will turn out well. As former New York City Mayor Rudy Guiliani said "... hope is not a strategy."

For the other *wanna-be* achievers, we fool, trick or tell ourselves that we are too busy to read, study and learn from others that have walked a similar path before us. But we have plenty of time to figure it out all by ourselves.

For the actual achievers who do not have time to waste and are living what they are achieving, we should ask them: Did they start off with a blank sheet of paper or did they find and follow a template to help them reach their goals and fulfill their dreams?

How do you see the difference between an achiever and a wanna-be achiever? Achievers are productive and achieve. Wanna-be achievers are busy and don't achieve.

For some people like me, it takes quite a while to get started with a blank sheet of paper. It is taking me years or even decades to learn how to use a *Blank Sheet of Paper* properly. Even today, I still don't know how to use it properly, but I am getting better.

Given a choice, I will always choose to work off a template rather than a blank sheet of paper, as the older I get the less time and energy I have to recreate what has already been tried, tested and proven to work.

Even songs have been written about how difficult it is to work with a blank sheet of paper.

American country singer/songwriter Tim McGraw wrote a song called *Blank Sheet of Paper*.

My takeaway: I don't want to wait until the end of my life to discover that I still am or mostly am a blank sheet of paper and to realize I had wasted the best years of my life not doing more, enjoying more and giving back more.

Chapter 2

Playing in the Sandbox!

"The mind is everything. What you think you become." —Buddha

From a very young age, I think children figured it out that it is more fun to play with someone else than to play alone. Constructive playing is also a great way to learn, grow and get stronger. Children learn better when they are having fun, and we can take learning to a new level or play a bigger game by keeping it entertaining and engaging.

I believe inside all of us still lives a child who likes to play. So what is the difference between a boy and man? Perhaps it is the size of their toys? "He who dies with the most toys wins" was a popular phrase coined by

Malcolm Forbes, who at the time was one of the richest men in the world. That phrase was probably centered around **Greed** or material possessions. If our lives are centered more about contributing instead of consuming, perhaps we will be able to live more harmoniously and happily together.

Depending on the game we play, and whom we play with or against, we can be growing, getting better and having fun at the same time.

Playing well is to play to your strengths and not your weaknesses. It is desirable to play an excellent game but more desirable to have game excellence. We can also take this concept or idea to working, investing or just living better.

Working and trying to get better at something we are not good at or told to be better at something we have no desire for is a sure recipe for frustration and unhappiness. Accelerating and sustaining growth comes from stretching in our areas of strength.

Some successful people stop when they reach their comfort zone in their areas of strength. That is a perfectly good zone to stay in, depending on our age and stage in life. The good zone to stay in is our strength zone. If we don't have one, we should figure it out, work on it, and getter better at it.

The least desirable place to operate is in our zone of weakness. Consider how we can identify our zones of strengths and weaknesses by studying the following diagram.

1. Danger Zone

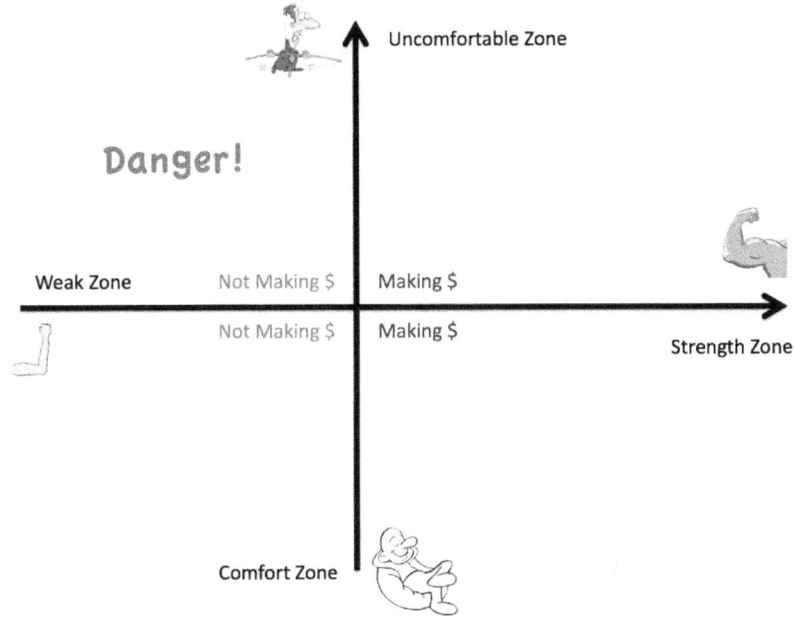

There are at least three reasons why people invest in the danger zone. First, it is an Ego thing or excitement or getting an adrenaline rush. Second, they are uninformed and have acted on bad advice. Third, is a *follow the herd mentality*. If everybody is doing it, it must be right, so I am doing it too.

Any reason for assuming unnecessary, uninformed and uncalculated risks in investing can be dangerous. Investing in something we do not understand can be unsafe, unwise and unprofitable. We will elaborate more about investing in the chapter titled *Car and Driver*.

We seem to have a fascination for excitement associated with danger. Regarding investing, I prefer a more mundane, predictable and pedestrian strategy for consistent results.

The character Jester from the movie "Top Gun" summarizes the Danger Zone investment strategy best with this one phrase:

Jester: "That was some of the best flying I've seen to date—right up to the part where you got killed."

2. Complacent

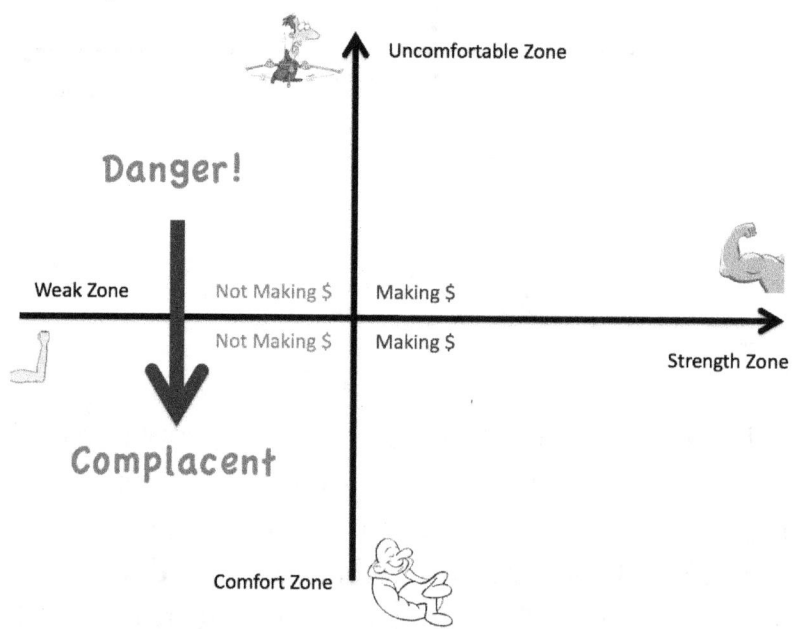

If we are fortunate to escape from the danger zone and enter a safe zone, we may have a tendency to let our guard down and start to get comfortable. Unfortunately, getting comfortable for too long can dull our senses, and we may become complacent.

Complacency is like tooth decay. When we do not make the effort to brush our teeth daily, our teeth will start to rot and decay. Brushing our teeth every day is an easy thing to do. Unfortunately, what is easy to do is also easy not to do.

What is the only part of the human body that is not able to repair itself? Your teeth.

"*Decay occurs without effort.*"—William Teh

3. Competent

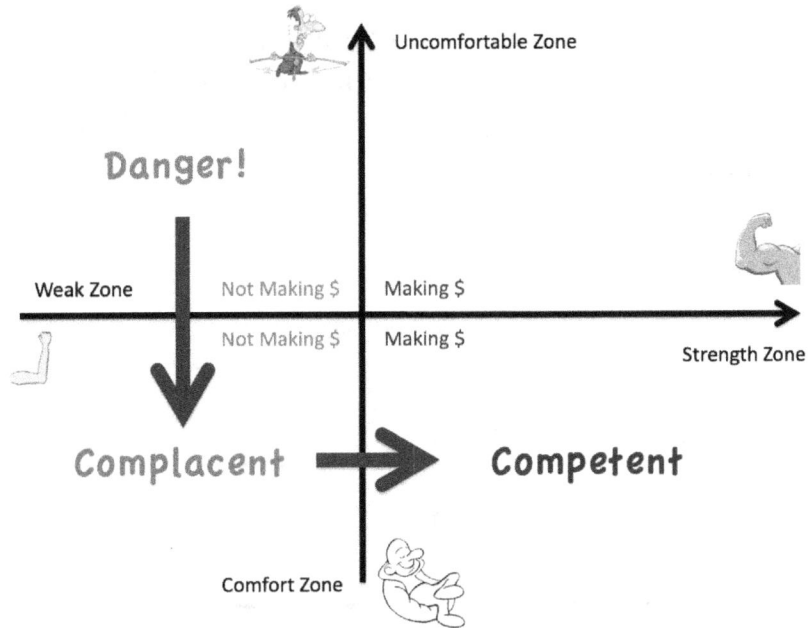

Google Dictionary's definition of competent is "having the necessary ability, knowledge or skill to do something successfully."

I like to think of competence as being the King of your hill, da Big Dog in your domain, or the Master of your sandbox.

How do we acquire competency? Competency comes with practice. In Chapter 1 of my earlier book *Choose Well. Live Better.* I talk about how it takes 10,000 hours of practice to become a Master at your trade or craft. How long will it take to get 10,000 hours of practice, study or work under our belt? About five years. Invest 40 hours per week for 50 weeks a year, and you will accumulate 10,000 hours in five years.

What happens after you acquire competency? First, you should become a Master at your craft. Second, you should be recognized as a professional at your craft. And third, as my mentor Dr. Nido Qubein, President of High Point University, says, "Competence leads to Confidence."

4. Growth!

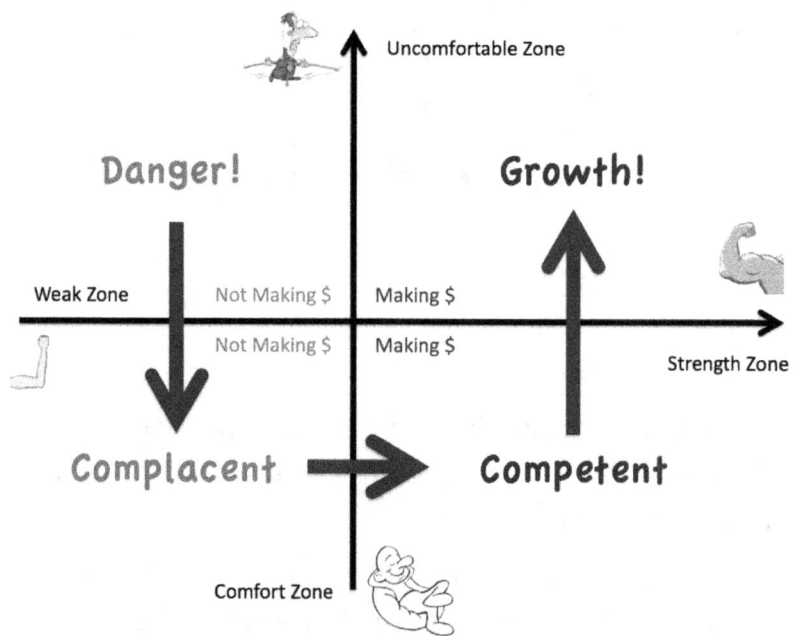

As we discussed earlier, being competent is being the master of your sandbox.

But what if we want to grow and play in a bigger or different sandbox? This is like moving from competence to growth.

What is a safe, secure and speedy way to move from playing in your sandbox to a larger sandbox?

Instead of organically growing your sandbox, it may be a lot easier, simpler and faster to befriend and play together with a bigger kid in a larger sandbox.

In the previous chapter we talked about using a template versus a blank sheet of paper to help us design our life. Playing together in your friend's larger or more desirable sandbox should complement the discussion of using a template versus blank sheet of paper to accelerate our Growth!

Summary

We started out in the danger zone with an "!" and we can evolve into the growth zone also with an "!"

"!" could mean crash and burn or "!" could also mean AMAZING!

Where we want to put the "!" in our lives is completely up to us.

> *"Where do you want to put the '!' in your life?"*
> —William Teh

Chapter 3

Lessons from an Ice Cream

"Desire is like eating ice cream."
—William Teh

Why do children of all ages from 1 to 100 love to eat ice cream? Ever wonder why every time you take a lick of ice cream it makes you feel so good? Ice cream is not only delicious; it also cools and relaxes you on a hot day. And get this—licking ice cream actually makes you happy!

Research performed by the Institute of Psychiatry in London tracked the brain activity of people eating vanilla ice cream. It was found that as soon as their participants licked ice cream, they noticed an immediate effect on the orbitofrontal cortex area of the brain. The orbitofrontal cortex is the pleasure center of the brain and is activated when people are enjoying themselves.

Here are three lessons I gather from enjoying ice cream.

1. Making Ice Cream ... can be a good dream

Here is what I think is a good dream.

Research concludes that all mammals dream. The purpose of dreaming still remains a mystery. Humans are special. We can take our dreams out of our heads, give birth to them and bring them to life.

When we put forth effort to realize our dreams, we can take the dreams out our head and bring them into the real world. Otherwise our dreams only come alive when we daydream or sleep. Just like the imaginary friends we had when we were young, nobody can see them except us. We have to give birth to a dream to bring it into the real world. The child of a dream is a realized goal. I have heard that a goal is a dream with a date. So giving birth to a dream also needs to have a timeline attached to it.

And the bigger your dream, the longer it may take for it to give birth, to become a realized goal. The normal pregnancy period for a human baby is 40 weeks, but the gestation period for an elephant is 95 weeks; that's more than double that of a human baby. So the bigger your dream, the longer it may take you to make it a realized goal.

According to the law of reproduction for mammals, it takes at least one partner to make a baby. It's the same to realize a dream; you can't do it by yourself. You can dream by yourself, but to realize your dream it'll take more than just you.

You have to be committed to your dream if you want to give birth to it.

> *"Being committed is like being pregnant.*
> *You either ARE or you AREN'T."*
> *- Darren Hardy*

Your partner can either help you realize your dream, or turn your dream into a nightmare. You can also turn someone else's nightmare into your dream. Who you are partnering or sleeping with actually determines if your dream will become a realized goal or nightmare.

A good dream can also be an asset. Investopedia calls an Asset a resource with economic value that an individual, corporation or country owns or controls with the expectation that it will provide a future benefit. That is a mouthful for me.

Robert Kiyosaki who wrote the book *Rich Dad Poor Dad* calls an asset something that puts money into your pocket. This I can understand.

Consider Haagen-Dazs. Reuben and Rose Mattus created Haagen-Dazs in the Bronx, New York, back in 1961. They started with only three flavors: vanilla, chocolate and coffee. In 2017, Haagen-Dazs' ice cream sales exceeded $2 billion. I think products or services that add value to children will tend to do well, as their parents or guardians will buy them for their children.

> *"Your dreams can make you rich if they can satisfy the desires of a lot of people."*
> *- William Teh*

2. Eating Ice Cream ... is an enjoyable Desire

What is desire? In my earlier book *From Scarcity to Abundance* we discussed what desire is in Chapter 2. Here I'd like to expand our discussion on desire and share what I've understood more about this feeling since then. Desire is doing something we enjoy.

"Desire is like eating ice cream."
- William Teh

Here are my three observations about desire as it relates to eating ice cream.

First, if you eat too much ice-cream, it will make you sick. The same applies to our desires. In healthy moderation, we can satisfy and enjoy our desires. In excess, we can become sick when we overindulge in our desires.

Second, if we use cash to pay for our ice cream, our desire is an expense.*

An expense is money flowing out of your pocket.

Third, if we use credit to pay for our ice cream, our desire is a liability.*

A liability is something that takes money out of your pocket.

What is the difference between a good Dream and Desire? A good dream adds value to people, and people will pay you for a taste of your dream. A good dream can be an asset.*

An asset is something that puts money into your pocket.

Unlike a realized good dream, generally we have to pay to enjoy our desires. It is not likely that someone will pay me to enjoy my desires. A desire is either an expense or liability.

Dreams and desires have at least one thing in common: we enjoy them. So depending on how you fulfill your dreams or desires, you can influence, impact or improve the lives of many or one (yours).

When our dream is to live our purpose, and this becomes our work, then our goals become milestones for this journey called life.

As I am now fortunate to pass the half-century milestone of my life, I am becoming more mindful to devote more of my remaining time with my friends, family and favorite people. I want to enjoy pouring my energy into their lives and vice versa. As they pour their energies into my life, I become more like them, so I am careful to watch what is being poured into me.

Satisfying my desires are all about me, whereas fulfilling a good dream can change, influence, impact and improve the lives of others. See the chapter *It's a Small World* for how Walt Disney's dream made and still makes so many children happy.

> "A good dream can feed you.
> But you always have to feed your desires."
> —William Teh

3. The Law of Ice Cream

> "The law of ice cream states that if you
> let your ice cream melt, it will make a mess
> and someone will have to clean it up."
> —William Teh

Not to get overly technical about temperatures and sorts, but ice cream melts and makes a mess if you don't finish eating it in a timely fashion. You will also get sticky fingers. I am talking about eating ice cream on a stick.

So what started out as enjoying an ice cream (a desirable pleasure) could turn into a mess if you don't figure out how to finish your ice cream in a timely fashion.

More importantly, you or someone else will have to clean up the mess that YOU made. Like a half eaten ice cream, a half eaten desire can turn into a mess.

I am trying to follow the footsteps of American author Dan Brown who wrote *The Da Vinci Code*. He said, "I am trying to write books that taste like ice cream but have the nutrition of vegetables."

Allow me to conclude this chapter by sharing a vacation story with you.

I never planned or even thought to visit Alaska. In chatting with Choon Ming, my ex-colleague from our engineering days and dear old friend of a quarter century or more, I learned one of the items on his bucket list was to take his wife to see the northern lights and glaciers.

I recommended they try taking an Alaskan cruise or jump into a giant floating bucket to knock out one of the items on his bucket list.

I thought it was such a good idea to see the glaciers and visit Alaska too that I invited Choon Ming to come visit with me for a while. Then both our families jumped on a plane, hopped on a boat, and went floating around the ocean to see some giant icebergs in Alaska. We also managed to eat some salmon.

Choon Ming had been thinking about visiting Alaska for over five years. After retiring from full-time employment, he was just looking for some meaningful part-time work to supplement or replace a portion of his income, while having somewhere to go and something enjoyable to do. He tried his hand at several assignments, but nothing was enjoyable or fulfilling.

As he says, "Working just for money is crap." Doing anything you don't like for more than 20 hours a week turns into drudgery. The daily grind was becoming more and more exhausting, so why not surprise his wife with a nice vacation to a faraway place?

We talked about it in 2016, and performed the trip in 2017. *A dream conceived five years ago took over a year to plan and prepare and less than eight days to perform and complete.*

My takeaway: *No problem can withstand the onslaught of sustained thinking. And get the right help from the right people. Like some things, it may takes longer to plan and prepare than to actually do it.*

On one of the shore excursions in Juneau, we visited the Glacier Gardens Rainforest. I'd like to share the story of how Steve and Cindy Bowhay realized their dream.

Steve and Cindy Bowhay, a husband and wife couple running a nursery operation, were looking to expand their business located in Juneau, Alaska. In 1994, the couple purchased 6 ½ acres of storm-damaged property from a local businessman to create what is today the Glacier Gardens Rainforest. The Glacier Gardens Rainforest is dotted with upside-down trees, known as *Flower Towers*.

So how did Steve and Cindy's dream, which started out as a nightmare, become a reality?

Steve, a landscaper by trade, bought the 6 ½ acres of land because he wanted to use the stream's water on the land for hydroelectricity to power new greenhouses. Their plan was to use the rest of the land to create a guided tour for visitors to enjoy both the beautiful landscape as well as the gorgeous view of Juneau that the Thunder Mountain rock face cliff offered.

When Steve and Cindy bought the property, it had major ecological issues as a result of a huge storm that occurred in the summer of 1984. This storm caused a massive landslide that released hundreds of tons of organic material from the 1,500-foot elevation of the Heintzelman Ridge on Thunder Mountain.

Steve also worked on developing the lower areas into landscaped gardens. He rented heavy equipment to arrange masses of soil, plants, trees and rocks dragged down the mountain from the 1984 landslide that occurred 10 years before they bought the property. So one person's nightmare (the local businessman who sold the property to Steve) became another person's (Steve's) dream.

During the last couple of hours when Steve was positioning a large boulder into place, he damaged the brand new excavator he was using. Now Steve's dream was quickly turning into his nightmare. That boulder, now known as *Steve's Rock*, is the centerpiece of one of the many waterfalls flowing through the gardens.

Steve was angry. Steve was frustrated. Steve was at a loss. A large and expensive repair bill was popping up like a nightmare for damaging the rental equipment. Steve got so mad that he picked up a large tree by its root ball with the equipment arm and slammed the inverted tree into the ground trunk first.

The tree did not splinter or break and the tree stuck in the ground upside down.

Steve sat in the excavator and felt his temper cool off as he stared at the roots hang from the root ball like vines on a petunia basket.

It only took Steve a moment to envision how to use the trees cleared from the property.

He would stick the trees upside down and call them *Flower Towers*.

Each *Flower Tower* is made by shoving a spruce or hemlock tree into the ground 5–7 feet deep, with the root ball pointing toward the sky.

So in a fit of anger, Steve discovered a new way to differentiate his nursery and new garden to attract visitors and tourists who would travel from faraway lands and pay to see his upside-down tree garden.

Today, Steve's dream employs over 60 people to take care of the garden and provides enjoyment to tourists and visitors who willingly pay to enjoy part of his dream.

Reader's Digest recognizes The Flower Towers as one of America's most interesting landmarks.

After our tour of the gardens, we stopped by the gift shop café to warm up with a cup of coffee and munch down a hot dog before heading on to the next excursion.

Walking around the gift shop, I spotted this lovely card signed by Steve Bowhay.

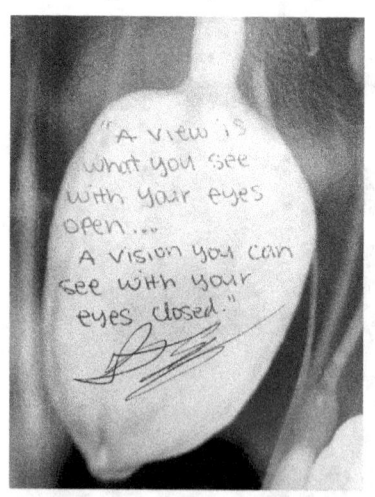

"A view is what you see with your eyes open ... A vision you can see with your eyes closed."
—*Steve Bowhay*

Opportunities are all around us. We can find them when we are able to manage our state correctly. How about using stress at work to take a faraway vacation or planting a unique garden because your rental equipment broke down?

Sometimes, in our darkest hour, it is in this time we can see the smallest spark of a new idea. When the lights are too bright or too many, we cannot find the spark.

"You can only see a spark of light in the dark."
—William Teh

Chapter 4

Lessons from a Beach Ball

"Nobody is perfect. That's why pencils have erasers."

Beach balls are inflatable balls used for beach and water games. Beach balls are characterized by their large size and light weight that take little effort to propel. Beach balls travel very slowly and generally must be caught with both hands.

Jonathon DeLonge is credited with inventing the beach ball back in 1938.

The beach ball is also recognized as one of the ALL-TIME 100 most influential toys. Imagine something as simple and inexpensive as a beach ball is still an all-time 100 most influential toy.

What can we learn from a Beach Ball?

Pushing a Beach Ball underwater

Have you ever tried pushing a beach ball underwater? It is a lot more difficult than you think. You need two hands. It is like the ball is alive and you have to constantly wrestle with the ball and the ball never gets tired. You need to focus all your effort to keep the ball underwater. The bigger the ball, the harder it is to hold it underwater.

My Takeaway:

Pushing a beach ball underwater does not seem like a meaningful task and takes a lot of energy and concentration. In my life, I try to find the "beach ball" (activities) I am pushing underwater.

Sometimes "I am pushing a beach ball underwater in my brain." This may be worrying or staying upset at something or someone who does not really care how we feel.

Pushing a beach ball underwater is really an unproductive activity.

Holding a Beach Ball with both hands

The average diameter of a beach ball is about 17". It is too big to be held in one hand securely. And since the beach ball is very light, the slightest wind or movement can cause it to waver and fall.

Although it does not take much effort, it requires both hands to securely hold a beach ball, leaving us with no free hands to do anything else.

A beach ball weighs almost nothing but takes both hands to hold it.

Try walking about and looking at people around you with your mind's eye. How many people can you see holding a beach ball with both hands? Being preoccupied with things so seemingly unimportant?

When I walk around I see so many people holding a beach ball with both hands in the shape of a smartphone. Their left hand is holding the phone, and their right hand is texting.

Sometimes I think a smartphone has more uses than it is designed for. A smartphone can act like a brightly colored beach ball. People hold on to a brightly colored beach ball that says, "Hey, look at me! See how important and busy I am!"

Or a smartphone can act like an umbrella or barrier. We use the smartphone to look preoccupied so as to avoid eye contact and make conversation.

These are the people who appear to look busy. Maybe it's because they are holding a beach ball with both hands?

When we are so busy performing a low-value activity, we don't have any hands left to do something better or notice what is going on around us.

Based on a study performed by professor Alejandro Lleras, at the University of Illinois psychology department, it was discovered that mobile device addiction is associated with depression and anxiety.

For some of us, we allow the digital world and our virtual friends to become more important than the real world and our real friends. This may cause self-inflicted problems.

Floating Beach Balls

Beach balls tend to be large and very light. They float easily on water and are almost completely above the water.

When two or more freely floating beach balls happen to bump into each other, they merely bounce off each other. And since they are so light, they hardly make an impact or are able to cause any damage to anything they bump into.

If people behave like beach balls instead of the so many Road Rage Warriors (drivers), wouldn't this be a much more pleasant place to live?

When people are behind the wheel of a car, it can give them a false sense of power or security and encourages them to behave more aggressively and angrily than normal. We sometimes do this behind the email security screen too. We can be less inhibited in what we say in an email than if we were to say it to a person's face.

Sometimes by having a false sense of security or power, the less considerate we feel we need to be.

Beach Balls Travel Slowly

So to get really technical, in fluid dynamics, drag (which is sometimes called air resistance) is a type of frictional force acting opposite to the relative motion of any object moving with respect to the surrounding fluid, whether water or air.

Since a beach ball is a relatively large object with very little weight, the force of drag on a beach ball is very high.

No matter how hard we try to punch, throw or toss a beach ball, it does not go very far, fast or in a straight line.

Some people are like beach balls. They just don't go or do what they are supposed to do, no matter how hard we encourage them.

Do you have any beach balls on your team? You may want to consider trading them in for a fastball.

> *"The chains of habit are too light to be felt*
> *until they are too heavy to be broken."*
> *—Warren Buffett*

Chapter 5

Lessons from a Carton of Milk

"People's minds are changed through observation and not through argument."

—Will Rogers

Here is a little history about milk. Drinking milk started around 7,500 years ago in Central Europe.

Humans are unique when it comes to drinking milk.

We are the only species on the planet that drink milk from another species like from a cow as well as drink milk past infancy.

Human babies are born with lactase. Lactase is the enzyme needed to digest lactose, a milk protein. We are programmed to lose our ability to produce lactase by the age of 3 or 4. Milk is not a natural food for adult mammals.

Lactose intolerance is proof that we are not designed to drink milk as we grow up. According to Genetics Home Reference – NIH (https://ghr.nlm.nih.gov/), it is estimated that approximately 65 percent of the human population has a reduced ability to digest lactose.

It is a nightmare for cows to produce milk for human consumption. A non-pregnant cow does not make any milk. So dairy cows are repeatedly impregnated and kept pregnant to produce milk. Calves are purposefully taken away from their mothers so that the milking process can take place.

When the cow is exhausted from constantly being artificially impregnated and can no longer produce enough milk, it is sent to the slaughterhouse to be ground up as hamburger meat. This is the unglamorous life of a dairy cow — hardly close to the happy smiling cows we see on TV, commercials and milk cartons.

To the rest of the world, one of the most American things to do is drink a glass of milk. But today, Americans drink 37 percent less milk than they did in the 1970s.

What can we learn from a Carton of Milk?

Besides the history of drinking milk, what can we learn from a carton of milk?

Expiration Date

We used to buy milk for our children when they were younger. I was always mindful to buy milk with an expiration date that was the furthest out. I felt that having a carton of milk with the expiration date further out meant I had a longer time to drink the milk before it went bad.

Also, at some grocery stores, they sell milk at a discount from its full price when the expiration date gets closer. This leads me to believe that the quality of milk is worth less as it reaches its expiration date. I also do not often see expired milk in groceries stores. This leads me to believe that expired milk should not be sold, and hence has less value.

What is the meaning of an expiration date?

According to Merriam-Webster, it is the date after which something (such as a credit card) is no longer in effect, or the date after which a product (such as food or medicine) should not be sold because of an expected decline in quality or effectiveness.

How can we apply the concept of expiration to living better?

Just like milk, most other things also expire. I believe things expire when they lose their value or usefulness. Things may also lose their value when our purpose changes and we do not have a use for them. For instance, the value of my snow blower is less valuable to me when I move to a place where it does not snow. Or I may have no use for my riding lawn mower with four cup holders when I move to high-rise apartment in the middle of a city.

Sadly, some relationships may also expire. We may enjoy spending time with people with whom we have a common history and enjoy revisiting the past together. But if all we do is only revisit the past while in our present, we cannot move on or move forward. This only eats up our time in the present with no foreseeable future together.

What if we seek out people who wish to have a desirable common future with us, and we spend time together with them? We are investing our time in the present to create a better future.

With respect to relationships, we can decide to build, deepen or shed them. The sooner we can figure out which bucket we want to put our relationship in, the better we can allocate our time and the happier we will be.

Three Types of Quality

From a carton of milk, I learn that there are three types of quality.

1. Acceptable Quality

When a carton of unopened non-expired milk is properly kept in a refrigerator, more likely than not the milk is of an acceptable quality. To test if the milk is acceptable, take a sip of it. It should both smell and taste good. The taste test is a good test.

> *"The taste test is a good test."*
> —William Teh

2. Unacceptable Quality

When milk is left out in the open and starts to smell or

curd up, or is kept past its expiration date, most of us would consider it to be unacceptable.

> *"To check for quality, taste it. Don't swallow."*
> —William Teh

3. Unknown Quality

What do you do with a cup of milk that you find sitting on a table or in someone else's refrigerator? Do you drink it? I would consider the milk to be of unknown quality.

> *"When in doubt, throw it out."*
> —William Teh

Keeping Things in the Dark

If, after reading the introduction to this chapter, you still decide to drink or buy milk for your children, this section may have a dual benefit for you.

Milk, when exposed to sunlight or very strong artificial light for long periods of time, loses some of its vitamins. The more light milk is exposed to, the more its levels of vitamins A, C, and some B vitamins are reduced.

Milk stored in clear containers let light in, which can destroy its nutrients. In three days, milk stored in a lighted diary case can quickly degrade, losing its vitamins. It breaks down quickly, causing it to spoil and create off-flavors and a sour smell.

The milk industry is very careful to protect milk from the adverse effects of light during processing and storage, and consumers keep milk in dark refrigerators.

Milk is packaged and sold in plastic jugs, glass bottles and paper cartons.

Milk packaged in cardboard or opaque cartons provides the best protection from light. Milk will tend to store, taste and keep better.

We can also apply the concept of keeping milk in cartons to living better. Just like milk, some things are better kept in the dark.

The most common good activity performed in the dark is charitable giving. This has been well discussed and is still practiced today.

Another common practice of keeping things in the dark has to do with secrets. Private conversations are exactly what they should be — private.

Some of the happiest or contented people I know are those who live quietly out of the limelight, or spotlight of publicity. These are the unknown millionaires.

> *"Some things are better kept in the dark."*
> —William Teh

Chapter 6

Car and Driver

"Think on Paper."
—*Jim Rohn*

When I was younger, I was more of a car guy. Not about getting under the hood and tinkering with the engine, but I absolutely loved driving a stick shift or manual transmission car. My desire was not top speed, but rather I get great satisfaction when I can shift the gears transparently and take corners well.

Now, being a family man with young children, my vehicle of choice is a minivan, a shoebox on wheels. I am hooked on those power sliding middle doors and 15 cup holders. And don't get me started on the fold flat third-row seats.

I think other drivers are more considerate to minivan drivers, as most minivan drivers like myself are parents trying to shuttle their children to school and after-school activities every day. Other drivers seem to be more kind and give way to let me into a lane when I put on my turn signal and stick my hand out of the window.

My family and friends who ride with me feel that I drive slowly. I don't know why. I regularly overtake gas stations, mailboxes, billboard signs and the occasional bicyclist.

But sometimes passengers riding with me sit with clenched teeth and are white knuckled and paralyzed until they can't even speak. "When is Papa going to arrive at the next gas station so I can go pee?!"

Also, nobody considers a minivan driver to be threatening or crazy, and so we generally do not attract much attention from other drivers or cops. This may even be truer when we have installed car seats and a DVD playing talking elephants, pandas and turtle movies. By the way, the pandas and turtles also practice kung fu.

For those of you who do not have children or watch cartoons, I highly recommend you consider getting *Kung Fu Panda*, *Teenage Mutant Ninja Turtles*, and *Horton Hears a Who!* when the time is right.

Now, let's get back to the part of our title containing the words *Car and Driver*. Car and Driver is an American automotive enthusiast magazine, first called Sports Cars Illustrated in 1955. In its early years, the magazine focused primarily on small, imported sports cars. In 1961, the editor Karl Ludvigsen renamed the magazine Car and Driver to show a more general automotive focus.

So what is a Car and a Driver? A car is a vehicle. A vehicle is used to carry people to their chosen destination. A driver is a person who operates and controls the speed and direction of the vehicle to safely get to its destination.

I often hear educated or financially savvy people say that a car is a depreciating asset. I was quietly confused — for decades. How can an asset depreciate?

For someone like me, when I was beginning to invest, I did not understand what a "depreciating asset" was and was secretly confused. Worse yet, I repeated what I heard to make myself sound *intelligent*.

I was pretty good at being able to fool people less informed than I was. I had meaningless conversations with people of the same or less intelligence about depreciating assets. What a crock of poop.

And then, I finally understood the meaning of the word asset from Robert Kiyosaki, a world-famous author best known for his book *Rich Dad Poor Dad*.

Here is the best definition of an *asset* that I know and now use: An asset is something that puts money into your pocket. And a liability is something that takes money out of your pocket.

How can we apply the concept of a *Car and a Driver* to investing?

The Car is the Investment Vehicle

A car is a vehicle that can take us to our physical destination. Similarly, an investment vehicle can take us to our *financial* destination.

Picking the right vehicle can take us to our desired destination. But we have to choose the destination. The vehicle cannot pick the destination for us.

Investment vehicles may include stocks, bonds and real estate.

The common feature between a real estate investment vehicle and a motorcar is that they both depreciate.

A car depreciates, or loses value over time. Unless it is a garaged collector's car, very few people would pay more for a used car compared to when it was new.

Like a car, real estate used as an investment vehicle also depreciates. The U.S. Tax law allows you to depreciate property when you use the property in your business or as an income producing activity. This depreciation tax benefit is applicable even though your property may be appreciating in value.

Real Estate investment vehicles and motor vehicles both depreciate, but in different ways.

Additional Discussion about Investment Vehicles

Riding in a vehicle driven dangerously or irresponsibly can cause stress, injury or death to its occupants.

The same can also be said for riding in an investment vehicle driven dangerously.

It all depends on the Driver.

The Driver is the Asset or the Liability

The asset is the person who gives us a check that we can deposit into our bank account.

If we engage third-party management to collect and manage our investment properties for us, it is the management company that is our asset.

If you manage your investment properties yourself, the tenants who pay rent are your assets.

If we buy and sell non-income producing properties, the realtor who sells the property for us is the asset.

If we invest in the stock market and use a broker or adviser, our broker or adviser is our asset.

Whoever is giving or making you money is the asset.

You can crash, get hurt or die when you get into a car accident. Accidents generally happen when the driver makes poor driving decisions.

Investment vehicles by themselves don't make you money. Picking the right investment vehicle driven by the right asset (person) will make you money.

So if you are the owner of the investment vehicle, and you hired a driver (someone to manage or drive the investment vehicle for you), your responsibility as the owner is to *turn the car keys* over to your asset to drive the vehicle for you.

You would be getting in the way of yourself if you tried to micromanage by trying to tell your driver *how* to drive the vehicle. Your job is to tell your *driver* where you want to go and when you want to arrive. One way to annoy your driver is to be a *backseat driver.*

With respect to real estate as an investment vehicle, your job as the owner of the vehicle is to make sure you have enough money to maintain the vehicle for your driver (asset) to drive.

If you are not driving the vehicle yourself, you should find and pay qualified and experienced people to drive the vehicle for you. You tell your driver where you want to go and when you want to arrive. You then let your driver take you there.

When and if your driver (asset) is not performing, and becomes a liability, your job is to fire the driver, find another driver, or drive the investment vehicle yourself.

Additional discussion about Drivers

When you make decisions about your money alone, YOU can be an asset or a liability. So if YOU are a liability, you should consider firing yourself and get out of the driver seat.

To make yourself an asset, consider investing in yourself. Get educated. Get coaching. Get connected with the right people.

Car (Investment Vehicle) and Driver (Asset) Summary

Regarding the car you pick, make sure you kick the tires on your car before buying it. Check to see if the car is large enough and capable of taking you to your destination, or bear in mind that you may have to trade up or out of your car when the time comes. Just make sure the vehicle you choose can take you nearer to your financial destination.

Regarding the driver you pick, make sure your driver has a valid driver's license, is qualified, and has the experience to drive this class of vehicle. The driver could also very well be you.

If you are carrying a bunch of passengers (e.g. investors) with you, it may be a good idea to have a co-driver or co-pilot to help you drive your vehicle.

Perhaps a more common phrase you may hear or get asked is, "What would happen if you got hit by a bus?"

Part of financial freedom is being able to do what you want to do with whom you want to do it, whenever you want.

If you have a qualified driver(s) driving your investment vehicles for you, you can let go of the steering wheel and sit in the back seat to enjoy the ride.

> *"What are your investment vehicles,*
> *and Who are your assets?"*
> —William Teh

Today, my favorite vehicle to drive on the road is a minivan. I sit up higher. I can haul my children around easily, and it is great for road trips.

But my favorite vehicle of choice to drive or ride to financial freedom is the BMW. The BMW rides quickly, comfortably and safely.

What is this BMW? BMW is a thought or due

diligence process I use to evaluate projects and their outcomes before committing time and money.

BMW is an acronym for:

Best Case Outcome:

If this project performed flawlessly, what is the Best Case Outcome I can expect to achieve?

Most Likely Outcome:

If this project performed as planned, with the usual or budgeted hiccups, what is the Most Likely Outcome I can expect to achieve?

Worst Outcome:

If everything did not go as planned, what is the Worst Case Outcome I can expect to achieve?

My takeaway:

If you are willing to accept the Worst Case Outcome for a chance to achieve the Best Case Outcome, Do it!

If you can't figure your BMW strategy, Drop it!

I would recommend a BMW as the preferred vehicle as we journey down the road of life.

And make sure you have enough gas (resources) to drive your BMW.

Driving at 2,000 Rpm

When we own a car, it is also important to bear in mind the longevity and reliability of the vehicle as well as its fuel economy, performance and other safety features.

The same can be said for the investment vehicles we drive.

Most modern-day cars have an engine that red lines around 6,000 rpm. Today, cars can comfortably cruise between 60–70 miles per hour at around 2,000 rpm. The engine generally has a reserve of 4,000 rpm to accelerate at any time.

The more starts, stops, and turns we do, the more wear we put on the engine, brakes and tires. The longer we cruise at a constant speed, the less wear and tear we put on the vehicle.

Much of what we know and understand about driving a car can also be applied to driving our investment vehicles. We can drive our vehicles aggressively or conservatively.

Examples of driving our investment vehicles to the red line may be applying excessively high leverage, overcharging prices or rent, and/or overworking your team. It is only a matter of time when driving our investment vehicle unnecessarily at the red line causes our vehicle to fail, stall or break down—usually at the most inconvenient time.

The problem with driving at the red line most of the time is the same as pushing ourselves too hard. People and cars are not designed to be driven at the red line all of the time.

Americans seem to be fascinated with being busy; they feel proud to be busy. I think some people equate being busy to being important. "Oh look how busy I am!"

Being busy all the time may be a cover-up for lazy thinking. If you had planned your day, week, month, or year better, you wouldn't be so busy and could still complete everything you need to accomplish.

> *"Being busy is a cover-up for lazy thinking."*
> —William Teh

James Autry and Stephen Mitchell who co-authored the book *Real Power: Business Lessons From the Tao Te Ching* tell us that managers have assumed that the successful businessperson tries to be everywhere at the same time and never wastes a minute. While driving, they talk on the cell phone. When in the hotel room, they go online with email. When on vacation, they're always in touch with the office.

When times are tough, they get busier. When things go wrong, they get busier. When things are great, they get busier. They are flattered when people describe them as very busy. And when someone says, "I hate to bother you because you are so busy," they take it as the ultimate compliment.

This is the way I understand *busyness*. If you are busy all of the time when times are bad or good, and you can't seem to get away from your job, then maybe you are not very good at what you do.

Being constantly busy is like living your life on the red line all of the time.

You are going to burn out, flame out or blow a gasket (get a heart attack!).

> *"To remain constantly at work will cause you to lose the power of judgment."*—Leonardo Da Vinci

Let me conclude this chapter by sharing with you a couple of differences between how people who stumble through life compare to those who are living with purpose.

#	Stumbling through life... ☹	Living with purpose... ☺
1	...are busy. Why? See #2	...are productive. Why? See #2
2	...try to do and be good at everything	...try to do well and be good at their ONE thing
3	...see success as a destination	...see success as a journey
4	... see feedback and coaching as someone criticizing them as a person	...know they have weak spots and seek out thoughtful criticism
5	...have unstructured energy	...have a focused system
6	...see making mistakes as discouraging and failing	...see making mistakes as part of growing and seasoning
7	...desire to be the strongest, smartest and fastest person	...surround themselves with people who are stronger, smarter and faster than them
8	...consider knowledge to be power and hoard it	...understand that knowledge is becoming a commodity and openly share it
9	... value learning from their own experiences and self-educating themselves, which costs them time and money	... value learning from other people's experiences and pay for coaching and mentoring, which saves them time and money

10	…go faster	…go further
11	…focus on being right	…focus on getting a better outcome
12	…show up when they feel like it	…show up every day
13	…blame others	…accept responsibility
14	…have complex, non-implementable solutions…	…have simple, implementable solutions…
15	that lead to inconsistent, unreliable, and non-reproducible results	that produce predictable, reliable and sustainable results
16	…value money over time and relationships	…value relationships and time over money

> *"Money you can lose and make back.*
> *But time you can only lose."*
> *- William Teh*

And finally, here is the chart of the Dunning-Kruger Effect.

Dunning-Kruger Effect

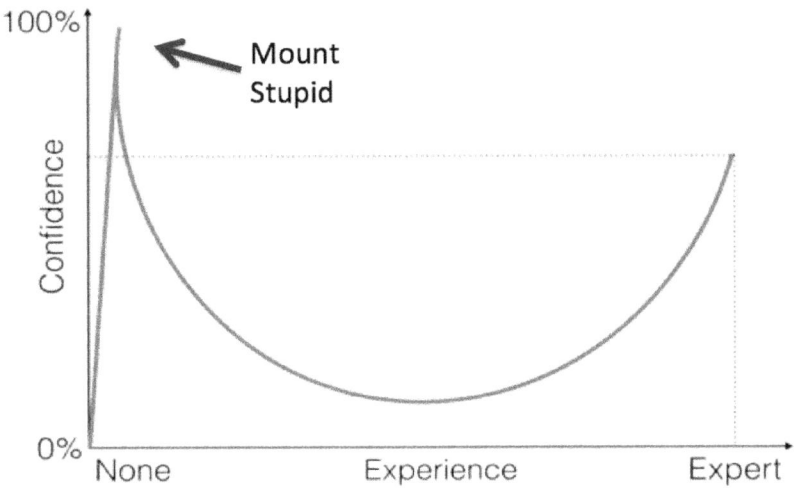

Dunning and Kruger do a nice job of demonstrating what it is like to be unskilled and being unaware of it. They show how difficulties in recognizing one's own incompetence can lead to inflated self-assessments.

Dunning, D. and Kruger, J. (1999)

"Mount Stupid" is where people who have a little knowledge and no experience reside. Seminar junkies are the ones who go to a couple of seminars and learn a few new words or acronyms. Then they leave, thinking they know everything. Book smart people are the ones who read a book or two, learn a few new words or acronyms, and feel they know everything. The common factor is that these people have no real life experience.

Mount Stupid can easily be summarized by this phrase:

"I know enough to be dangerous."

Chapter 7

It's a Small World

Our greatest natural resource is the minds of our children."
—Walt Disney

Have you been or taken your children to Disneyland Park or Walt Disney World? My favorite attraction is and still is the "It's a small world" ride.

You hop on a boat and float through different lands where over 300 animated doll children dressed up in their traditional costumes from their culture will sing, dance and perform "It's a small world" for you. "It's a small world" has a theme of global peace. According to Time.com, "It's a small world" is the most performed song of all time.

"It's a small world" ride has been open since May 28, 1966, and still remains one of children's and parent's favorite rides at Disneyland and Walt Disney World. Here's a fun fact that you may not know. When the ride first opened at Disneyland, Walt Disney invited children from all over the world to visit the city of Anaheim to help dedicate the ride. The children brought containers of water from rivers and seas of their native lands. This water was added to the beautiful waterfall that is inside the attraction.

Legend has it that once you experience "It's a small world" at Walt Disney World or Disneyland, the song will forever stay in your head. "It's a small world after all … It's a small world after all …"

The happiest part of the attraction for me is getting on the boat after waiting in line for over 45 minutes for a 15-minute ride. The saddest part of the ride is getting off.

The best part of the experience is journeying through the lands. The destination is the same place where we got on, except we get off on the other side of the boat when the ride ends.

So which is more enjoyable? The journey or the destination?

What did we really pay for? The ride or getting to the destination?

Sometimes, arriving at the destination may not be the ultimate goal, especially if we end up exactly where we started.

For the longest time, I never really understood the difference between financial security and financial freedom. I thought they meant the same thing.

Perhaps we can try to use the concept of destination versus journey to better understand financial security versus financial freedom.

Financial Security is a Destination

Most people's financial destination or goal is to achieve financial security so that they can retire comfortably. Financial security is generally a future event. If retirement is tied to financial security, then retirement is also a future event.

Financial security is about picking investment vehicles or instruments to grow our nest egg. If things go well, then after about 40-plus years of *feeding* the egg, our egg will hopefully be large enough to sustain us through retirement until we Rest In Peace (RIP).

It is a strong probability that if we stay in the financial markets long enough, we will experience financial turbulence. When the ride gets bumpy, eggs get rolled around, bounced around and possibly take a knock or two — and may even crack.

The biggest problem with investing for financial security is that it is a future event. We have to keep feeding the egg.

We are advised not to eat the egg while we are feeding it, as it may not grow big enough to support us when we retire. We may be so busy feeding and taking care of the egg that YOU (the poor chicken) are too exhausted, worn out, and tired to enjoy your egg while you are able to because you are always working to feed it.

For most people, retirement and achieving financial security are future events — a place we can reach if we live frugally, save hard, and live below our means.

Financial security advisers tell us that we can get by on less money after we retire. For those of us lucky enough, we can retire frugally after a lifetime of working 40 hours per week for 40 years on 40 percent of our income for the rest of our life. This is the 40-40-40 rule that most of our parents, grandparents and financial planners teach us.

I generally only hear three types of advice from financial advisers: 1) live below your means; 2) get out of debt; and 3) defer retirement as long as you can so you will not have to eat into your nest egg. Most financial advisers teach their clients how to achieve financial security, not financial freedom.

So the perfect destination and journey regarding achieving financial security is to: work for a lifetime living below our means; save enough money to live frugally in our retirement years; and if we timed it perfectly, we bounce the last check we write to the undertaker.

How many of us give up the best years of our lives to prepare to *JUST* survive in our old age by adopting the financial security strategy?

> *"A man should never neglect his family for business."*
> *—Walt Disney*

There are at least three problems with investing for financial security. First is having a financial adviser tell me when I can afford to retire. Second is having someone tell me that I need less money to live on (have a lesser quality of life) after I retire. And third is that I know of some lucky friends who have retired using the financial security strategy and they still worry about having enough money to sustain them until they RIP.

People adopting the financial security plan primarily focus on cutting costs and rarely focus on learning how to increase their means or income.

Instead, I'd like to welcome you to the world of Financial Freedom. Financial Freedom investors focus on generating the right kind of income.

> "You reach a point where you don't work for money."
> —Walt Disney

Financial Freedom is a Journey

Financial Freedom can be a present event. It all depends on the type of income we generate to achieve financial freedom.

In my earlier book *From Scarcity to Abundance* I discussed how I understand financial freedom from the Greek letter Pi (π).

I believe we can achieve financial freedom when our Passive Income (Pi) is greater than our expenses. Passive income is any income that we do not have to work to earn. Passive income is doing the right things once and getting paid over and over again.

Earned income is trading hours (our time) for dollars. Earned income is getting paid only when you show up for work. You only get paid once each time you show up.

We achieve Financial Freedom when our Passive Income is greater than our expenses.

Financial Freedom = $\dfrac{\text{Passive Income}}{\text{Expenses}} > 1$

Achieving, protecting and maintaining a Financial Freedom ratio of > 1 is a constant process.

Just like life, the ratio of Passive Income to our expenses is a living and constantly changing number.

Generally, the higher the quality of life we wish to lead, the higher our expense load will be.

We discussed the three concepts of Pi in my earlier book "From Scarcity to Abundance" and so we will not repeat it again here.

How we generate our income is more by design or choice, then working the design to generate the income.

Saving and investing for financial security is not the same as saving and investing for financial freedom.

We can spend a whole lifetime working to achieve financial security and never achieve financial freedom. The financial security plan is to convert as much of our earned income into savings within a portfolio of investment vehicles (our nest egg) and hope that over time it will be big enough to sustain us till we RIP.

Working toward financial freedom is about generating an infinite stream of passive income that is greater than our monthly expenses. If we do it right, the stream of passive income can continue to can carry on after we are carried away. Wouldn't it be nice to leave something like that for our children, and wouldn't it be nicer to receive it? Key for recipients are to learn how to manage and take care of the financial freedom assets and vehicles to continue the stream of passive income.

Investing for Financial Security and Financial Freedom are not the same disciplines.

Financial security is building up a nest egg. We start eating the nest egg after our primary source of income (usually earned income) dries up after we retire.

The problem with investing for financial security is worrying about having too many days left at the end of the month, once we start eating our egg. For some people, the journey and destination to financial security generally ends up being centered on always working, feeling worn out, and constantly worrying about not having enough. I have also heard it said this way; maximum security is the same as minimum freedom.

Financial freedom is like growing and maintaining a herd of milking cows. Our cows are our investment vehicles that throw off passive income or cash flow (milk). Our assets are the farm hands we hire to look after our cows. (See the previous chapter, Car and Driver, for discussion of investment vehicles and assets.)

> *"Financial Security is a future event.*
> *But Financial Freedom can be a present event."*
> *- William Teh*

We can't plan and achieve financial freedom today when we only work and save for financial security tomorrow. This is like trying to find a sunrise looking west.

"You cannot find a sunrise looking west."
—William Teh

And finally I believe ...

"Having money can buy you freedom or imprison you. But lack of money will always imprison you."
—William Teh

Chapter 8

Who is Paying for Lunch?

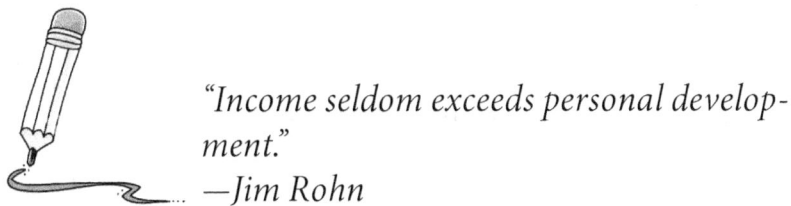
"Income seldom exceeds personal development."
—Jim Rohn

About once a month I try to catch up and eat lunch with my good friend Gene. The lunches we eat may be considered by many to be rather long and leisurely.

It takes a while for the wait staff to understand how slowly we eat lunch, even though we go to the same place, come at the same time, and eat the same food.

Once they figure out our eating habits, feeding and taking care of us is easy as pie. Come to think about it, we have yet to eat a slice of pie together, and our favorite food is Pi.

Pick up my earlier book *From Scarcity to Abundance* and read the chapter on *What is Pi?* for a complete discussion on Pi.

Let's use the discussion of who really pays for a leisurely, long lunch to introduce the three different types of Income, three different types of Investors, and three different types of lifestyles.

Three types of income

1. Earned Income

This is the way I think about earned income. I am paying for lunch when I am making money from earned income. Otherwise, the most common definition of earned income is income derived from paid work, or trading time for dollars.

> *"I am paying for my lunch when I am making money from Earned Income."*
> —William Teh

Why do they call April 1 April Fool's day? We call it April Fool's day because most of us have to work into April to pay our federal and state taxes. In 2018 that day was April 19th and is called *Tax Freedom Day*. Earned income also has one of the highest tax rates along with short-term capital gains.

There are a couple of challenges with using earned income to pay for our living expenses. First, if we depend solely on earned income to pay for our living expenses, we are completely dependent on our health, ability and availability to work. When we stop working or producing, our earned income will eventually dry up.

Another problem with earned income is that it always seems to get in the way of our recreation or family time.

> *"If you don't find a way to make money in your sleep, you will work until you die."*
> —Warren Buffett

2. Portfolio Income

This is the way I think about portfolio income. The stock market is paying for my lunch when I am making money from portfolio income. Otherwise, a common definition of portfolio income is income derived from investments, dividends, interest earned and capital gains.

> *"The market is paying for my lunch when I am making money from my portfolio income."*
> —William Teh

In the United States, depending on when you take profits, portfolio income can be taxed at your personal income tax rate or at the more favorable long-term capital gains rate (U.S. is currently the 6th highest in the world). Almost always the long-term capital gains tax rate is more favorable than your personal income tax rate.

But there are some countries that are more investor friendly and do not have capital gains tax. Presently, the United States is not one of them.

There are a couple of challenges with using portfolio income to pay for your living expenses. First, if you depend solely on portfolio income to pay for your living expenses, you would require a substantial amount of capital to generate enough returns to cover your monthly expenses. Second, from my experience I always seem to have the worst timing whenever I need to withdraw money to pay for my expenses.

3. Passive Income

This is how I think about passive income. Someone else is paying for my lunch when I am making money from passive income. Otherwise, a common definition of passive income is income derived from rental income, limited partnerships, or enterprises in which a person is not actively involved.

> *Someone else is paying for my lunch when I am making money from passive Income."*
> —William Teh

There are a couple of common phrases to describe passive income. Warren Buffett calls it making money in your sleep. If we have rental income as part of our passive income stream, we call that mailbox money.

More commonly, investors call it buying *assets* that generate positive cash flow. It is buying investment vehicles managed by *assets* (people) that throw off passive income.

There are several advantages of investing for passive income over the other types of income.

One advantage is the ability to use leverage. We can leverage time and money. We can hire people or professionals to manage our investments for us. We can borrow money from a bank to help us buy investment real estate.

Passive income is usually the most sheltered form of income, or the least taxed income in the United States.

Another advantage is the ability to force appreciation. We can force the appreciation of our investment vehicle (real estate or business) by increasing its operating income.

We can also pick the asset (people) we engage to drive our investment vehicle, hence having more control over our investments.

One of the challenges about investing for passive income is that it is a slow process, and some people do not have the patience or time to build up their passive income to exceed their expenses. It takes a different mindset, skill set and education to generate passive income.

Three types of investors

1. Savers

Savers are people who live below their income level. Their primary mode of saving is to spend less than they make. They generally do not know how to make more money as they are limited by their time, skills and mainly unwillingness to take risks. Savers are risk adverse. Savers hate taking risks. If they invest, they invest in what they consider to be safe investment vehicles. They buy Certificates of Deposits, commonly known as CDs.

Today, we call them Certificates of Deaths because the returns are so low that they can't keep up with our cost of living. If savers invest in the stock market, they buy mutual funds or hold a highly diversified portfolio basket of stocks.

Savers diversify because they do not take the time to get educated and generally let someone else manage their finances or investments. Savers rely on time in the market to make their returns.

The biggest challenge for savers is not to save more or to cut more expenses, but rather to learn how to grow their income. There is a floor to how low we can cut our expenses. But there is no ceiling as to how high we can grow our income.

> *"It's more important to grow your*
> *income than cut your expenses.*
> *It's more important to grow your*
> *spirit than cut your dreams."*
> *—Robert Kiyosaki*

2. Speculators

Speculators take more control over their investments than savers do. They also do not solely rely on time in the market to reach their financial goals. Speculators tend to invest more time studying the markets and investments, and hence also tend to be more financially educated than savers. As a result, speculators have a better understanding of opportunities and underlying risks, making higher returns in a shorter period of time.

Speculators make their money by being at the right place at the right time and taking the right actions.

3. Specialists

Da Specialist! The specialist does not diversify. A specialist hedges their risks and opportunities. The specialist studies and picks his investment vehicles carefully. The specialist understands that to make superior returns on his investments it's all about education, experience and engaging the right team. With this approach, the specialist differentiates himself by offering a better value, providing better service, and generating superior returns.

Speculators need to be at the right place at the right time to take the right action to be successful. Specialists differ from speculators in that they focus on being at the right place ALL of the time, while taking the correct actions.

Specialists can generate superior returns on their investments with less risk using this strategy.

> *"Specialize until you are special."*
> *—Dr. John C. Maxwell*

To conclude the section about investing, I believe and embrace what all my personal development and wealth mentors say: "The FIRST investment you should make is to invest in YOURSELF."

Warren Buffet tells us, "Never invest in a business you can't understand." So first invest in yourself to get educated.

Three ways to live

An enjoyable lifestyle depends on how you invest and

the type of income you generate. The type of income we generate will also determine how much time we have to enjoy it.

1. Survive

This is the most undesirable type of life to live. We try to scratch out a living getting by day by day, never sure about our next meal. It is very stressful constantly worrying about having too many days at the end of the month before getting paid again.

Survivors also hope to save enough to retire after a lifetime of working or punching the clock.

The typical advice financial advisers offer is that we should aim to replace 70–90 percent of our annual pre-retirement income through retirement income, investments, savings and Social Security. My question is this: When we retire from a job, and have at least 40 hours a week returned to us by not having to work, shouldn't we use this time to explore, experience and enjoy all the activities we postponed because we previously did not have the time, energy or money?

The strategy of working for a lifetime, living below our means, and saving for retirement seems to be a failing strategy for most people.

Just take a look at this chart published by the Bureau of Labor Statistics *(Bureau of Labor Statistics/ Older workers: Labor force trends and career options/ Mitra Toossi and Elka Torpey/ May 2017).*

By 2024, BLS projects that the labor force will grow to about 164 million people. That number includes about

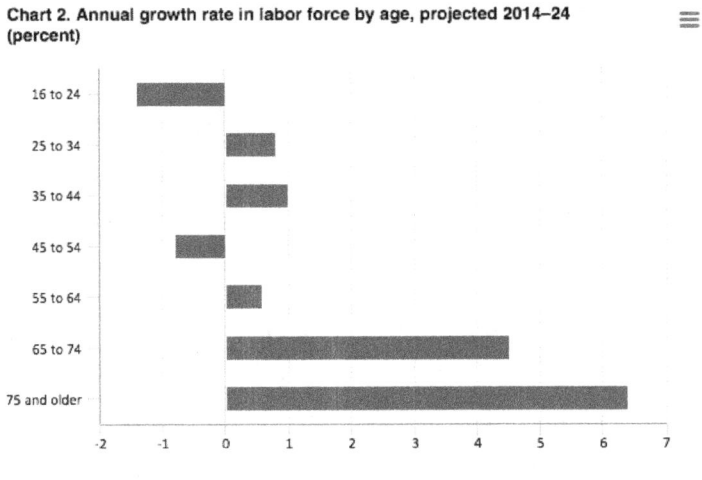

41 million people who will be ages 55 and older—of whom 13 million are expected to be ages 65 and older.

So between looking at the chart and what BLS is telling us, this is what I understand. The fastest growing employment segment by age group is comprised of people 75 years and older.

By 2024, about 25 percent of the American workforce will be 55 years of age or older.

If working and saving to retire were effective strategies, then why is the highest job growth by age 75 and older?

Shouldn't we—after the age of 55—be thinking and planning where to take nice vacations, watch the grass or grandchildren grow (if we have any), or volunteer to give back to our communities?

I think saving for retirement is a failing strategy. Perhaps we should save to invest for passive cash flow and let our passive cash flow investments carry us as we watch the grass and grandchildren grow, if we have any.

2. Success

Those of us whom have achieved success through hard work appreciate the value of labor. Here is the caveat as explained by Napoleon Hill in his book "Truthful Living: The First Writings of Napoleon Hill":

> *"No matter how big your pay, if you do not make yourself independent of hard work, self-control, and saving—independent of job and employer—you are nothing but your employer's slave. He owns your TIME, and HE who owns your time OWNS YOU."*
> —Napoleon Hill

For those of us fortunate enough to have made enough, we can enjoy the luxury to consume the products and services we desire for an easier life.

The unfortunate thing about simply living a life of ease is that it generally does not last forever.

People who stumble across large sums of money usually do not keep it, or more correctly, lose it. Lottery winners, gamblers at the casino or stock market winners, or children who receive a big inheritance all at once, seldom keep their money for a long period of time.

What do they say? Easy come easy go? If we do not grow into our income, we will generally not get to keep it.

Sports Illustrated recently estimated that 80 percent of retired NFL players go broke within their first three years after leaving the League.

> *"Get rid of your poor habits. They will make you broke."*
> —William Teh

3. Significance

When I study some of the truly wealthy people, I observe that they focus on adding value first, then being compensated for the value they add.

> *"The great and glorious masterpiece of man is how to live with purpose."*
> —Michel Eyquem de Montaigne

Conclusion:

When trying to design your life, remember to consider designing the type of income you want generate. How you generate your income greatly influences how much time and energy you will have to live your desired lifestyle.

As we wind down this chapter, Gene is fighting me to grab the lunch check, as we know that neither one of us is really paying for the meal.

Chapter 9

One Worm Does Not Make a Can

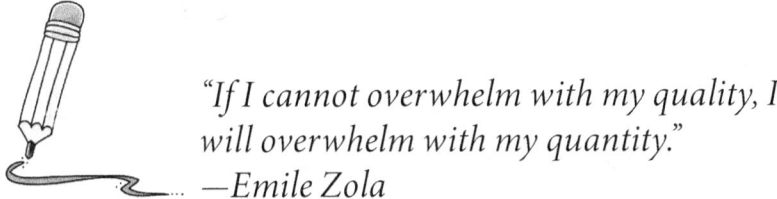

"If I cannot overwhelm with my quality, I will overwhelm with my quantity."
—Emile Zola

Have you heard the expression, "Opening a can of worms"? This involves attempting to solve a problem followed by an action or a set of actions that creates a whole separate set of problems that were not there in the first place.

The exact origin of the phrase is not completely known, but the general thought is that it traces back to the United States from the 1950s.

Evidence suggests that the original cans of worms were real cans with actual worms in them, collected as bait for fishing.

So I understand that opening a can of worms to be creating unnecessary work. If you were expecting this chapter to talk about a can of worms in the same context as creating unnecessary work, then you are misled.

The context and content of this chapter revolves around investing. Allow me to use a can and worms to help me explain how I view investing.

One worm does not make a can

This is how I think about one worm not making a can. With respect to investing, I think of a worm and a can as:

Worm(s)   = our deal(s)

Can   = our pipeline of deals

When I think about investment deals I think about: deal flow, deal quality and deal size.

We invest to make money. We are in the business to make money by solving problems. We are not in the business of inheriting problems.

Deal Flow

Deal flow is a term used by financial professionals such as venture capitalists, angel investors, private equity investors, and others to refer to the rate at which they receive business proposals or investment offers.

Deal Quality

Deal quality is the ability to find good deals that can be successfully monetized.

Great opportunities usually don't find us. We have to seek them out.

Mike Collier, founder and chairman of Get Rich Steady, taught me that great opportunities usually have one or more of these characteristics:

- It is a hidden asset
- It is an overlooked opportunity
- It has underperforming activities
- It has undervalued relationships
- It has underutilized distribution channels.

Deal Size

Deal size is about buying the right size deal for my partners and me. One of the main questions is, "Does the deal have enough critical mass to throw off the desired cash flow or returns for the effort we invest into the deal?"

I am mindful that it takes a lot of work to find the right deal, scrub the deal, and raise capital to successfully close on the deal and make money.

Generally, the amount of time and effort to take down a larger deal is the same as a smaller deal. There are only a few more zeros behind each number you look at.

In the commercial real estate investment space, sometimes it may be more risky to purchase deals that are too small if you are buying them to hold for cash flow.

When the deal is too small, it may not throw off enough cash flow to engage third-party management to manage the property, and you'll end up having to do much of the work yourself. A couple of vacancies can also make the deal go upside down in terms of generating positive cash flow after paying for operating expenses and servicing the mortgage if you have one.

This defeats the goals of buying commercial property for the purpose of generating passive income to free you up to enjoy having the free time to do what you want, with whom you want, whenever you want. That's one of the fruits of financial freedom.

Using these three criteria, I am mindful to treat investing as a business and not as a hobby. I try to pick only qualified people to participate in the deal. These people include contractors, investors and partners.

To conclude this chapter, I'd like to share 13 worms and a can of wisdom with you.

13 Worms and a Can of Wisdom

1. One worm does not make a can.
2. Treat your worms nicely.
3. Worms are blind. They don't find you. You have to find them.
4. Skinny worms eat more than fat worms.
5. There are good worms, bad worms and dead worms.
6. There are more bad worms than good worms.
7. You can die eating too many bad worms.
8. How quickly can you pick out a good worm? See #9.

ONE WORM DOES NOT MAKE A CAN

9. **You have to lick a lot of worms to find a good worm.**
   How small a lick do you need to taste a bad worm? The more worms you lick, the smaller a lick you'll need.
10. Don't share your worms with frogs.
11. Don't fall in love with your worms.
12. Everybody knows "The early bird gets the worm."
13. And finally …
    Get the right help to open your can of worms.

"One worm does not make a can."
—William Teh

Acknowledgment:

I'd like to recognize my good friend and investor Jim Licata. I appreciate our dialogues, discussions and lively debates that helped me develop the material for "One worm does not make a can."

May I complement the material in this chapter by discussing how we can become a MASTER at picking good worms out of a can?

From my earlier book *13 Ways to Accomplish More by Doing Less* we wrote about how to use the MASTER strategy to invest successfully.

Since then, I use the MASTER template or strategy to analyze business opportunities. After learning from a couple of unsuccessful projects, I added another step to the MASTER template. By incorporating this additional step, I think the strategy is much better.

Here is a shortened version of the MASTER strategy with the additional step.

M: Market

Pick a desirable market you wish to invest in.

A: Analyze

Analyze your market. Is your market big enough to support your sales to generate your target amount of profit or cash flow?

S: Strategy

Develop your strategy to serve your chosen market. The better you serve your market, the better your profits and cash flow will be.

T: Test

Test your strategy. This is the additional step I have included in my MASTER template. Before we totally commit our resources and energy into serving our market, it would be prudent to pilot test your strategy. Test your market. Test your team. Test your product or service.

T: Team

Develop your team to help you serve your market. Consider team players that have the right skill set, experience and knowledge to be on your team. Their attitudes, values and ability to work with other people will determine whether you maintain or fire them. Your team will either Make or Break you.

E: Execute

Execute or take action. Nothing happens without acting on your strategy.

R: Results

Measure your results. If we are not hitting our numbers within a reasonable period, we should consider exiting our project or position. We can set our own exit criteria or have someone help us.

To trace where I may have made a mistake, I always begin with the end in mind first.

If I am not getting the desired results, I first check to see if I am executing the plan properly. If not, I fix how I am executing the plan. If I am working the plan properly and still not getting the desired results, then I back up one step.

Are your team members' strengths properly aligned

to their tasks and responsibilities? If not, fix your team. Either hire better people or put your people in their right places. If your team is not the problem, back up two steps.

Is your strategy sound? Did you do a good test? If not, fix your strategy and retest. Otherwise, back up another step.

Did you analyze your market correctly? Did you miss something? If your analysis is inaccurate, reanalyze your market. Otherwise back up another step.

Has your market changed so much that you are not profitable or don't have cash flowing properly? If the answer is no, then the problem is YOU. You have not read or anticipated the market correctly or developed a robust MASTER strategy.

If the market has changed significantly, the problem is also YOU. You are not paying attention to your chosen line of business by watching and anticipating your market. You have probably fallen down into the trenches doing busy work (execution activities) that your team should be doing, usually because a member of your team is not performing well. The RIGHT thing to do is to find and replace that member on your team. Refresh you mind again by re-reading the chapter on *Lessons from a Beach Ball*.

> *"You can't coach from the benches
> when you are down in the trenches."*
> —William Teh

So at the end of the day, when your projects are not performing up to their expectations, the buck stops with YOU.

Chapter 10

Don't Eat that Cookie

"People need to be reminded more often than they need to be instructed."
—Samuel Johnson

Have you noticed that when we are told not to do something, we are sensitized to it, tend to pay more attention to it, and want to try it?

Say for example there is a box of freshly baked different cookies on the table, and someone tells me, "You can eat any cookie in the box except this one. Don't eat it." Just because you told me not to eat it, it drives me crazy and I want to eat that one!

It has been part of human nature since the beginning of mankind.

Let us refresh our minds with a couple of stories from the past to help us understand why we just can't stand being told not to eat a cookie.

Here is a well-known story about Adam and Eve eating the forbidden fruit (commonly known and referred to as the apple) in the garden of Eden. Let's refresh our minds with that story.

Adam and Eve

The Creation of Man and Woman

2 Thus the heavens and earth were completed, and all their hosts. By the seventh day God completed His work which He had done, and He rested on the seventh day from all His work which he had done. Then God blessed the seventh day and sanctified it, because in it He rested from all his work which God had created and made.

This is the account of the heavens and earth when they were created, in the day that the Lord God made earth and heaven. Now no shrub of the field was yet in the earth, and no plant of the field had yet sprouted, for the Lord God had not sent rain upon the earth, and there was no man to cultivate the ground. But a mist used to rise from the earth and water the whole surface of the ground. Then the Lord God formed man of dust from the ground, and breathed into his nostrils the breath of life; and man became a living being. The Lord God planted a garden toward the east, in Eden; and there He placed the man whom He had formed. Out of the ground the Lord God caused to grow every tree that is pleasing to the sight and good for food; the tree of life also in the midst of the garden, and the tree of the knowledge of good and evil.

Now a river flowed out of Eden to water the garden; and from there it divided and became four rivers. The name of the first is Pishon; it flows around the whole land of Havilah, where there is gold. The gold of that land is good; the bdellium and the onyx stone are there. The name of the second river is Gihon; it flows around the whole land of Cush. The name of the third river is Tigris; it flows east of Assyria. And the fourth river is the Euphrates.

Then the Lord God took the man and put him into the garden of Eden to cultivate and keep it. The Lord God commanded the man, saying, "From any tree of the garden you may eat freely; but from the tree of knowledge of good and evil you shall not eat, for in the day that you eat from it you will surely die."

Then the Lord God said, "It is not good for the man to be alone; I will make him a helper suitable for him. Out of the ground the Lord God formed every beast of the field and every bird of the sky, and brought them to the man to see what he would call them; and whatever the man called a living creature, that was its name. The man gave names to all the cattle, and to the birds of the sky, and to every beast of the field, but for Adam there was not found a helper suitable for him. So the Lord God caused a deep sleep to fall upon the man, and he slept; then He took one of his ribs and closed up the flesh at that place. The Lord God fashioned into a woman the rib which He had taken from the man, and brought her to the man. The man said,

> *"This is now bone of my bones,*
> *and flesh of my flesh;*
> *She shall be called Woman,*
> *Because she was taken out of Man."*

For this reason a man shall leave his father and his mother, and be joined to his wife; and they shall become one flesh. And the man and his wife were both naked and were not ashamed.

The Fall of Man

3 Now the serpent was more crafty than any beast of the field which the Lord God had made. And he said to the woman, "Indeed, has God said, 'You shall not eat from any tree of the garden'?" The woman said to the serpent, "From the fruit of the trees of the garden we may eat; but from the fruit of the tree which is in the middle of the garden, God has said, 'You shall not eat from it or touch it, or you will die.'" The serpent said to the woman, "You surely will not die! For God knows that in the day you eat from it your eyes will be opened, and you will be like God, knowing good and evil." When the woman saw that the tree was good for food, and that it was a delight to the eyes, and that the tree was desirable to make one wise, she took from its fruit and ate; and she gave also to her husband with her, and he ate. Then the eyes of both of them were opened, and they knew that they were naked; and they sewed fig leaves together and made themselves loin coverings.

They heard the sound of the Lord God walking in the garden in the cool of the day, and the man and his wife hid themselves from the presence of the Lord God among the trees of the garden. Then the Lord God called to the man, and said to him, "Where are you?" He said, "I heard the sound of you in the garden, and I was afraid because I was naked; so I hid myself." And He said, "Who told you that you were naked? Have you eaten from the tree of which I commanded you not to eat?" The man said, "The woman whom You gave to be with me, she gave me from the tree, and I ate." Then the Lord God said to the woman, "What is this you have done?" And the woman said, "The serpent deceived me, and I ate." The Lord God said to the serpent,

> *"Because you have done this,*
> *Cursed are you more than all cattle,*
> *And more than every beast of the field;*
> *On your belly you will go,*
> *And dust you will eat*
> *All the days of your life;*
> *And I will put enmity*
> *Between you and the woman,*
> *And between your seed and her seed;*
> *He shall bruise you on the head,*
> *And you shall bruise him on the heel."*
> *To the woman He said,*
> *"I will greatly multiply*
> *Your pain in childbirth,*
> *In pain you will bring forth children;*
> *Yet your desire will be for your husband,*
> *And he will rule over you."*

Then to Adam He said, "Because you have listened to the voice of your wife, and have eaten from the tree about which I commanded you, saying 'You shall not eat from it';

> *Cursed is the ground because of you;*
>
> *In toil you will eat of it*
>
> *All the days of your life.*
>
> *"Both thorns and thistles it shall grow for you;*
>
> *And you will eat the plants of the field;*
>
> *By the sweat of your face*
>
> *You will eat bread,*
>
> *Till you return to the ground,*
>
> *Because from it you were taken;*
>
> *For you are dust,*
>
> *And to dust you shall return."*

Now the man called his wife's name Eve, because she was the mother of all the living. The Lord God made garments of skin for Adam and his wife, and clothed them.

Then the Lord God said, "Behold, the man has become like one of Us, knowing good and evil; and now, he might stretch out his hand, and take also from the tree of life, and eat, and live forever." Therefore the Lord God sent him out of the garden of Eden, to cultivate the ground from which he was taken. So He drove the man out; and at the east of the garden of Eden He stationed the cherubim and the flaming sword which turned every direction to guard the way to the tree of life.

Adam was the first man that God created, and he was very special. Adam was created in the image of God Himself.

God planted a beautiful garden, the garden of Eden. It

had beautiful trees with delicious fruit — everything a person would need to eat. Right in the middle of the garden was the tree of life and the tree of knowledge of good and evil. Then the Lord God took the man and put him in the garden of Eden to work it and take care of it. And the Lord God commanded the man, "You are free to eat from any tree in the garden; but you must not eat from the tree of knowledge of good and evil, for when you eat of it you will surely die."

Adam was all alone in the garden with no one to help him. So God put Adam into a deep sleep and took one of his ribs and formed it into a woman to be Adam's wife. Adam named her Eve.

The Serpent

Of all the animals God created, the serpent was the most tricky and deceitful. He came to Eve and asked, "Really? None of the fruit in the garden? God says you must not eat from any of it?" "Of course we can eat it," Eve replied. "It's only the fruit from the tree of knowledge of good and evil that we cannot eat. God says we mustn't eat it or ever touch it, or we will die."

"That's a lie!" said the serpent. "You won't die! God knows very well that when you eat it you will become like Him — you will know good from evil." Eve looked at the fruit on the tree of knowledge of good and evil and saw that it looked fresh and delicious. She thought the fruit would make her wise like the serpent said it would. Eve was convinced. She picked the fruit and ate it, and she gave some to Adam to eat too.

Genesis Chapter 2–3 (New American Standard Bible version)

Trying not to eat a cookie placed in front of my face is like trying to fight a losing battle. Like the alien group Borg in the Star Trek: The Next Generation series says: "Resistance is futile."

I think it may be oversimplifying to put curiosity into the same bucket as *sin*. Curiosity is a hallmark of intelligence and not sin.

The more common understanding of sin is performing an immoral act considered to be a transgression against a divine law. I think of sin to be more along the lines of intentionally causing harm or hurt to another without just reason or cause.

A better way to eliminate what we consider undesirable behavior is to design an environment where that behavior cannot be demonstrated. I believe the best preventive solution is to completely take away the *cookie*.

Perhaps a less well-known story (at least to me) is the story of Pandora's box.

Pandora's Box

The story of Pandora's box begins with the story of Zeus, Prometheus and Epimetheus. Prometheus and his brother Epimetheus were Titans but pledged their loyalty to Zeus and the Olympians. Prometheus was born with the special power of prophecy and knew that Zeus would defeat the Titans. Zeus rewarded Prometheus and Epimetheus for their loyalty and gave them the job of creating the first creatures to live on Earth.

Epimetheus formed the animals and gave each a special skill and form of protection. Prometheus took his time molding man, and was left with no forms of protection since Epimetheus had already given them away. Prometheus knew man needed some form of protection and asked Zeus if he could let man have fire. Zeus refused. Fire was only for the gods. Prometheus ignored Zeus and gave man fire anyway. For this, Prometheus was punished. Zeus tied him with chains to a rock far away in the Caucasus Mountains where nobody would find him. Every day Zeus sent an eagle to feast upon Prometheus' liver, which grew back every day so that Prometheus would have to endure this torture daily until Hercules found Prometheus and killed the eagle and let Prometheus go.

This torture wasn't enough of a punishment for Zeus who also believed that humans should be punished for accepting the gift of fire from Prometheus. To punish man, Zeus created a woman named Pandora. She was molded to look like the beautiful goddess Aphrodite. She received the gift of wisdom, beauty, kindness, peace, generosity, and health from the gods.

Zeus brought her to Earth to be Epimetheus' wife. Even though Epimetheus' brother Prometheus had warned him of Zeus' trickery and told him not to accept gifts from the gods, Epimetheus was too taken with Pandora's beauty and wanted to marry her anyway.

As a wedding present, Zeus gave Pandora a box (in ancient Greece this was called a jar) but warned her never to open it. Pandora, who was created to be curious, couldn't stay away from the box, and the urge to open the box overcame her. Horrible things flew out of the box including greed, hatred, pain, disease, hunger, poverty, war and death. All of life's miseries had been let out into the world. Pandora slammed the lid of the box

> back down. The last thing remaining inside the box was ... hope. Ever since, humans have been able to hold onto this hope in order to survive the wickedness that Pandora had let out.
>
> Pandora's box now means anything that is best left untouched, for fear of what might come out of it.
>
> www.greekboston.com

So what I learned from a box and an apple are that some things never change. From the beginning of mankind until today, we supposedly (as a social, intelligent and curious people) like to try the unknown, test our boundaries, and unconsciously make trouble. Curiosity is the left foot of intelligence.

By the way, were you able to pick out some similarities between both stories?

Exercising discipline or restraint is not a winning or sustainable formula for most people and is generally frustrating when we are told we can't, shouldn't, or must not do something that we want to try or do.

To complete the discussion of the cookie, allow me to share a third story. It is a Buddhist story about Ananda's Temptation.

To be a Monk or a Husband

> Buddha had many disciples during the years; many of whom had achieved enlightenment. And many had powerful or inspiring stories on their journey with the great teacher.
>
> This was especially true of Ananda, one of the first monks of Buddha. Ananda had come from a wealthy family, but

when he met Buddha, he knew he wanted to follow him.

Ananda, the Handsome

According to ancient texts, Ananda was a handsome man who attracted a lot of attention from women. Of course, this was a problem because he was a monk, and monks usually don't have girlfriends (in case you didn't notice).

One day, Ananda was begging in a city and on the way back he saw a well. Next to this well was a beautiful woman. Ananda was thirsty, so he asked for a drink. The two got to talking, and it was obvious she felt an attraction to him.

Ananda left, but he realized he was attracted as well. This confused him. But he went about his business, not thinking too much of it.

The next day, he went back into the city, and the same girl was there; only this time, she had a new dress and hairdo. She grabbed him and refused to let him go.

This was now a difficult situation — what should he do?

Confused, he went back to Buddha and told him everything.

"Bring the girl to me," he said..

The Agreement

Surprised, Ananda went back to the village and told the girl.

She agreed, although she was nervous. But she would do almost anything to be with Ananda. When they came before Buddha, he asked a pointed question towards the *girl: "Ananda is a practiced monk. To be his wife, you must leave home for a year and become a nun. Are you willing to do that?"*

"Yes, I can do that, lord Buddha." She was surprised that there was no resistance. "You must get approval from your parents."

She immediately left and asked her mother, and she agreed. Buddha made it very easy for her to come into the circle of disciples, and she undertook all the normal rituals: she shaved her head, did the practices Buddha recommended, and followed his guidance.

She faithfully served Buddha and became a model nun. Many in the community looked up to her.

The Beginning of a Path

After a year, Buddha came to her.

"Are you ready to marry Ananda?" he asked.

"I have given it a lot of thought, but I have decided I feel complete where I am. I see now you knew it wasn't the right path for either of us."

There was a pause. Then Buddha simply nodded. When Buddha talked to Ananda about it, he agreed as well, saying, "Since following this path, I have known my place is here. I want to be a monk."

Both of them lived long lives and achieved enlightenment. Their stories became well known in Buddhist history.

By Matt Caron

Reflecting on these three stories, I think there are at least three options to eat or not to eat a cookie.

DON'T EAT THAT COOKIE

	First, if we must eat cookies, eat them in moderation or responsibly.
"We only make pies here."	Second, if cookies are bad for you, just don't make them.
"Have a carrot."	My third and best option is to replace the cookie with something better.

Chapter 11

From Muda to Madu

"We used a pencil when we were young. Now we use a pen. Why? Because mistakes made during our childhood can be more easily erased, unlike now."

Muda (むだ) is a Japanese word for futility, uselessness or wastefulness. It is a key concept in the Toyota Production System.

Toyota identified seven wastes in their production. See how we can use or eliminate these seven wastes from eating up our time.

1. Transportation:

Definition: Moving products that are not actually

required to perform the processing.

Each time a product is moved, there is a risk of it being damaged, lost, or delayed, as well as being a cost for no added value.

Transportation does not make any transformation to the product that the consumer is willing to pay for.

My Take on Transportation Waste

Performing unnecessary tasks entail doing things that do not add value or contribute toward our objectives. When we are unclear about what we need to accomplish, we end up doing things we like without making progress toward our cause. It is wasteful.

Another way of thinking about this is stirring a cold pot of soup and not making it taste better.

2. Inventory:

Definition: All components, work-in-process and finished products not being processed.

Inventory may be in the form of raw materials, work-in-progress (WIP), or finished goods representing a capital outlay that has not yet produced income, either by the producer or for the consumer. Any of these items (raw materials, WIP or finished goods) not being actively processed to add value are waste. The smooth and continuous flow of work through each process ensures that the excess amount of inventory is minimized.

My Take on Inventory

An inventory of stuff that we do not use or cannot use only takes up space. An inventory of data and information that we do not use takes up space in our brain. An inventory of bad memories and feelings takes up space in our heart and saps our energy.

By keeping unnecessary inventory, we increase the probability of losing stuff, waste time finding stuff, and make it more difficult to move stuff around. In a MANUFACTURING environment, we learned to keep Just-In-Time (JIT) inventory. But most of us keep Just-In-Case inventory.

In a LIFE environment, I think the three types of desirable inventory to accumulate are: 1) Free Time, 2) Free Space, and 3) Happy Choices.

Accumulating and maintaining these types of inventory is a constant and never-ending process of continuous improvement.

Having an ample supply of these three types of inventory can help us act sooner, respond faster, and even slow down aging! Why? Because these are the basic ingredients to make a good H.A.M. (Happiness. Abundance. Memories.).

When we have our priorities aligned with our purpose, we can start appreciating, acquiring and accumulating the right kinds of LIFE inventory.

3. Motion:

Definition: People or equipment moving or walking more than is required to perform the processing.

In contrast to transportation (which refers to damage to products and transportation costs associated with moving them), motion refers to damage that the production process inflicts on the entity that creates the product, either over time (wear and tear for equipment and repetitive strain injuries for workers) during discrete events (accidents that damage equipment and/or workers)

My Take on Motion

Activity is not the same as Accomplishment. Acting or looking busy is wasted motion. It just makes us tired. Just because we are moving, it does not mean we are making progress. It is just like riding a rocking horse: we're looking good but going nowhere.

4. Waiting:

Definition: Waiting for the next production step.

Whenever goods are not in transport or being processed, they are waiting. In traditional processes, a large part of an individual product's life is spent waiting to be processed.

My Take on Waiting

They say, "Good things come to those who wait." But it will be the leftovers from those who hustle. Waiting is not the same as preparing or priming. Waiting is an idle activity. Preparing is getting ready or setting up; it is priming the pump to burst into action when the time is ready. Those who are still waiting will be caught flat-footed.

5. Overproduction

Definition: Producing ahead of demand.

Overproduction occurs when more products are produced than are required at the time by your customers. One common practice that leads to this muda is the production of large batches. Often, consumer needs change over time, and the product become undesirable or obsolete. Overproduction is considered to be the worst muda because it hides and/or generates all the others. Overproduction leads to excess inventory, which then requires the expenditure of resources on storage space and preservation—activities that do not benefit the customer.

My Take on Overproduction

With respect to investing, I think about overproduction as being similar to over committing. Overproduction occurs when we make more than the market or our clients need or want. At the end of the day, we are stuck with too much inventory that we can't sell. The inventory costs us money to store and depreciate and may eventually become obsolete.

Over committing may be putting too many of our eggs in one basket or over leveraging.

We overproduce or over commit when we do not understand, do not listen, or are unresponsive to the market we serve. Over committing can be a result of ego, greed or taking bad advice from an unqualified source.

In the chapter "One worm does not make a can," we talked about the MAST2ER strategy. The second letter T represents Testing. We can Test the market by first making or offering samples before committing to full production. This will help keep us from over producing.

Also, don't get caught being cheap or greedy. Yes, I can get my price per piece cost down if I make a lot more. But what will happen if our customers are not willing to buy from us?

6. Over processing

Definition: Resulting from poor tool or product design creating activity.

Over processing occurs any time more work is done on a piece than is required by the customer. This also includes using components that are more precise, complex, of higher quality, or more expensive than absolutely required. (The traditional notion of waste is exemplified by scrap that is a result of poor product or process design.)

My Take on Over Processing

Investing too much time, energy and money into a deal that will not work or pay off is generally a result of treating investing as a hobby instead of a business. We are trying to make the numbers work instead of listening to the numbers. Beginning with the end in mind first can help us not to over process our deals.

Better to figure out if we can sell what we make at a profit before we commit to making something that no one is willing to pay for. Take for example, Real Estate — over improving the value of a fix and flip home way above the price the market expects or is willing to pay for. Working together with qualified cross-functional team members to assess the deal is also critical to minimizing the costs of over processing.

7. Defects

Definition: The effort involved in inspecting for and fixing defects.

Whenever defects occur, extra costs are incurred reworking the part and rescheduling production. This results in labor costs and more time in WIP. Defects in practice can sometimes double the cost of one single product. This muda should not be passed on to the customer and should be taken as a loss.

My Take on Defects

Defects are like mistakes. Nobody intentionally buys mistakes. Mistakes are the potholes and tree roots that trip us up; they are the rocks that block our way. To be in business for the long haul, we need to consider mistakes as our friends. Mistakes will always be there, and we can make them our enemies or our friends. Better to make them our friends. Make them early. Make them fast. Make them small. And finally, make them only Once.

Those who choose to view mistakes as enemies will usually fumble, fail, fall, and not be able to get up.

Making a defect once is a mistake. Making the same defect twice and not doing it again is a learning experience. Making the same defect three or more times is a — Choice.

Madu:

Madu is the Indonesian word for honey.

When you have Madu (honey), you can accomplish at least three things.

Honey Attracts Bees

Bees eat honey. Bees do work. Your responsibility is to feed the bees honey, not do the work.

Honey Attracts Bears

We talked about the salmon and the bear in my earlier

book *From Scarcity to Abundance*. I'd like to refer back to the bear characteristic again here.

Bears like to eat. The first thing on a bear's mind in the morning when it wakes up is FOOD.

Follow the FOOD principle of the bear and you will eat well. The FOOD principle is a four-step strategy to make decisions.

Here is the FOOD summary.

F_acts: Gather the facts

O_bservations Make your own observations from the facts.

O_pinions Form your own opinions. More importantly, seek the opinions of a qualified person(s) to help you solidify your opinions.

D_ecide Decide after you have chewed your FOOD.

Enjoy the Honey (Madu)

I consider enjoying Madu (honey) as having time, money and good health to do the things we like to do. The more Muda (waste) we produce, the less Madu (honey) we have.

A simple way to find YOUR Madu (honey) is to smell the Madu (honey) that someone else is already enjoying.

As you identify and eliminate the Muda's (waste) in your life, you can start to find and taste your Madu (honey).

The faster you can eliminate your Muda's (waste), the sooner you can enjoy your Madu (honey).

Chapter 12

Say the Number!

"You can't depend on your eyes when your mind is out of focus."
—Mark Twain

The abacus system of mental calculation is a system where students mentally visualize an abacus to perform calculations. An abacus is a simple device used to make manual mathematical calculations by sliding counters along rows of wires set inside a frame. By using the mental visualization technique, math calculations can be made at great speeds.

In 2012, champion Takeo Sasano was able to add 15 three-digit numbers in under two seconds at the Flash Anzan event at the All Japanese Soroban Championship.

There is more to just learning how to perform mathematical calculations using the abacus.

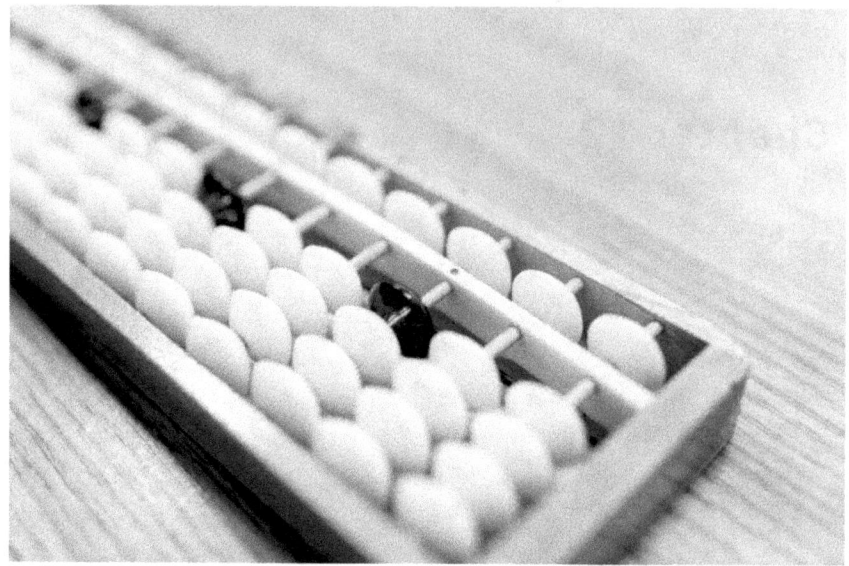

Students can acquire astonishing calculation speeds. However, the end results are achieved by developing these mental abilities:

- Concentration
- Visualization
- Observation
- Memory

At the time of this writing, my children and I are taking abacus classes at the Austin Abacus Brain Gym. Our instructor, whom we fondly address as Ms. V., teaches the course.

My only regret in learning abacus is starting too late. But I am glad I started. I keep dropping beads in my brain when I have to do mental abacus in image form. Doing abacus in image form is holding the abacus in my brain while visualizing pushing the abacus beads in my mind. I hope my children will not share my same regrets.

As Ms. V. says, "Abacus is not about learning math. Abacus is about learning mental visualization, focus and concentration."

Progression through abacus class works like this: We start with grade 10 and then complete the course when we reach grade one. This takes approximately five years.

I'd like to share three teaching phrases that Ms. V. uses in a rather firm voice to encourage her children (students) to better grasp the concepts of learning abacus. There are more phrases Ms. V. uses, but these are the three that stick best in my mind.

Say the Number!

Starting out in grade 10, Ms. V. teaches how to add and subtract two one-digit numbers. My biggest challenge is letting go of how I learned to add and subtract numbers, and doing it the abacus way, by pushing beads on the abacus. Then we have to do it in image. Image abacus is mentally visualizing the abacus in our head, pushing the beads in our mind, while keeping track and remembering the positions of the beads in our brain.

Graduating to grade nine we start to learn how to add and subtract two two-digit numbers. Things are starting to get really interesting now that we are learning to manage numbers using the second and third column of beads (10s and 100s).

Every time we get the numbers messed up or have our answers off by 10 or 100, Ms. V. will firmly remind us, "If you just SAY THE NUMBER, you will get the answer!"

The practice of *Say the Number!* is backed up by Edgar Dale's Cone of Experience (1969) where he concludes that we remember about 90 percent of what we learn when we hear, say, see, and do a task.

So …

"Say the Number!"

Today!

Our class with Ms. V. is on Thursday nights. Ms. V. is totally committed, dedicated and passionate about teaching abacus to her children. She teaches six days per week and only takes Fridays off. Ms. V. teaches one class per night from 6 p.m. to 8 p.m. on weekdays and two to three classes on Saturdays and Sundays. Every class runs for about two hours. Ms. V. dedicates almost her whole weekend to teaching abacus.

How does she do it? Ms. V. keeps a tight schedule, and she lives her life one-half hour at a time. Ms. V. blocks her calendar in blocks of half hours. An hour lunch is two one-half hour blocks. A two-hour class is four one-half hour blocks. I couldn't do it. That's why Ms. V. is Ms. V.

> *My takeaway: Live your life one-half hour at a time if you want to get more done.*

We go to classes on Saturday mornings to get extra help and time with Ms. V. Whenever Ms. V. notices a child(ren) becoming distracted or mind wandering off, she'll firmly remind the child(ren) to get back to work by firmly saying, "Today!"

Doing an important task at hand immediately is a good way to kill procrastination. It also helps when you get a reward. Like getting to go home.

So begin ...

"*Today!*"

Again!

Learning math the traditional way primarily requires using the left logical side of our brain. Learning math the abacus way requires using our right creative side as well as our left logical side of our brain.

Doing image abacus is keeping the picture of the abacus in our mind while virtually pushing the abacus beads in our mind with our fingers in the air. The younger we start learning abacus, the easier it is to do image abacus, as we do not have to unwire (unlearn) and rewire (relearn) our brain for manipulating numbers the abacus way.

Sitting in on Ms. V.'s advanced Saturday morning classes and watching her students (who are the same ages as my children Nathan and Hannah) multiply two four-digit numbers in their heads is testimony that abacus brain training works. They just started earlier.

Just watching Ms. V.'s advanced class students perform image abacus in their brains is like what Nathan describes as Black Magic. But in reality this is how Darren Hardy describes mastery: Amateurs call it genius. Masters call it practice.

"Mastery: Amateurs call it genius. Masters call it practice."
—*Darren Hardy*

Norman Vincent Peale said, "Repetition of the same thought or physical action develops into a habit which, repeated frequently enough, becomes an automatic reflex."

This is the same for doing math using the abacus method. If I have to think about how to move the beads to perform a math calculation, I have not mastered the abacus technique. The way Ms. V. checks for mastery is to constantly reduce the time to perform the calculations to the point where there is no time to think. You just move.

The magic starts to happen when the left-hand side of the brain holds hands with the right-hand side to push beads in our mind with little to no thinking.

To achieve Mastery, do it …

"Again!"

Additional discussion about *Today*

Mochamad Asri is a good friend who overcame many challenges to pursue his Ph.D. in Electrical and Computer Engineering at the University of Texas, Austin.

At the time of this writing, Asri is finishing his degree and has already secured a job to work for Apple. As hardworking, smart and intelligent as Asri is, he jokingly says that he only understands and deals with Zero's and One's.

Asri deals with limiting circumstances with unlimited thinking, copes with scarcity by making abundant choices, and gets comfortable being uncomfortable. Here is one of Asri's stories. To test and push his physical boundaries, Asri decided to participate in the 2018

Austin marathon. Asri prepared and trained for three months to run the race. This is what he told me as he was cramping up at mile 18 running the marathon:

> "There are many days to fail. Today is not the day."
> —Moch Asri

What we are able to do (perform) today is usually a result of months, years or decades of preparation. After a couple of months of traveling, thinking and tossing the thought around in my head, I'd like to paraphrase Asri's comment:

> "There are many days to give up. Today is not the day."

Regarding *giving up*, American actor Shia Saide LaBeouf tells us that if we don't want to start over again, don't give up.

Is there a time when it is good to give up? Yes, I think for at least these three situations.

The first thing to consider giving up is being perfect. Here we are referring to being perfect with respect to peer pressure. Keeping up with the Joneses in America or the Lees in Asia can be a major source of being unhappy. Will Rogers said, "Too many people spend money they haven't earned to buy things they don't want to impress people they don't like."

> "Too many people spend money they haven't earned to buy things they don't want to impress people they don't like."
> —Will Rogers

The second thing to give up is expecting everything to turn out perfectly. This is an almost guaranteed receipt to unhappiness. Perhaps our academic grading system is a main driver for this source of unrealistic or unreasonable expectations. Life is not like school. Who hands out perfect grades for the subject called Life?

Most of the time, we cannot control what happens to us, but we can always control how we respond to what happens to us.

I understand that there are two kinds of weather. We cannot control the weather outside, but we can always control the weather inside our heart. Stop trying to control the outside weather. Instead, pack an umbrella, sunglasses and a coat and have a *perfect day*!

The third thing to give up is to give up on hanging onto a mistake. Sometimes it may cost more to make it right, or prove you are right than to just let it go. As my legal counsel reminds me, "How much do you want to spend to prove that you are correct?" It may cost you an arm and a leg, a life, a friend, or an empty bank account.

> *"Don't hang on to a mistake just because you spent a lot of time and money making it."*
> —Unknown

Let me conclude this chapter with a story.

Very shortly after Nathan and Hannah were born, I stopped giving stuff as birthday presents to my children. Instead, I replaced gifts with vacations. In seventh grade Nathan got out of school a week earlier than Hannah. To encourage him to get good grades, I offered him a day of camping for every good grade he received instead of a physical gift. Nathan liked that.

After exploring camping equipment, and understanding my lack of skills and experience camping, my desire to go camping was fading quickly, especially understanding how much work it takes to take down and put everything away after a camping trip.

My wife Sandra understands my complete inability to be handy, so she suggested I take Nathan for a boy's trip instead. I jumped at it. I asked Nathan where he would like to go. He suggested visiting Yosemite National Park in California. I said, "OK." Ms. V.'s abacus class is every Thursday evening. We planned to leave on Friday morning and return on Wednesday so that we didn't have to miss her class.

Since starting abacus class with Ms. V., we've begun to take a little homework with us on our vacation trips so that we don't get too rusty when we return. I don't want Ms. V. to have to call me out to, "Say the Number!"

I enjoy doing Ms. V.'s abacus homework together with Hannah and Nathan when we are on vacation. Nathan is usually the fastest. And when I forget an abacus computation rule, I check with him and he reminds me *AGAIN!*

On this trip, whenever we had an opportunity to eat a more leisurely breakfast or dinner, we practiced doing Ms. V.'s abacus homework while waiting for our food. Nathan can normally complete the work faster than I can. When I complete my questions, we compare answers. For questions that we do not get the same answer, we redo the question. Usually one of us gets the right answer, and we get the same answer whenever we redo the question. It is always more fun to do abacus homework together, especially when we generate some interested looks and inquiries from the diners.

However, there was one thing that happened on this vacation that broke my heart.

We arrived at Mariposa, California, late Saturday night. Sunday morning we went into town to eat breakfast before heading into Yosemite National Park to play for the day. We picked The Sugar Pine Café because it had a high number of positive Yelp reviews.

We chose to sit at the counter so that we could watch Robert the cook prepare breakfast. Robert was very organized and able to keep everything in order. From turning over hash browns and pancakes to cooking custom-made eggs (from sunny-side up to over easy) to plating the meals, Robert did it all. Seeing Robert work was like watching him dance with the grill.

My takeaway: An expert makes things look easy.

Then we started working on Ms. V.'s homework.

As usual, Nathan knocked out his homework questions before I did.

As he was waiting for me to finish, Hannah texted me and asked us what we were doing. I texted back, "We are doing abacus while waiting for breakfast."

I also reminded Hannah to do her abacus homework.

Hannah texted back with a picture of her doing her abacus homework at home, and what she said brought a lump to my throat.

> *"Papa, are you happy that I am doing my abacus?"*
> —Hannah Teh

Just like Nathan and me, my little Hannah was doing her abacus homework after breakfast at home — except by herself.

Fast forward a week later, we are on summer vacation in Costa Rica. This is what we are doing together after breakfast.

Now I am happy.

Chapter 13

Full of Emptiness

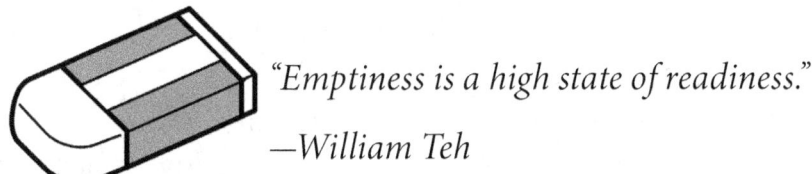

"Emptiness is a high state of readiness."
—William Teh

First we learned to use a piece of paper to capture our designs and thoughts. Then we learned to use a pencil to process and execute our thoughts. Here we learn to keep an eraser handy to make corrections to either the process or the design. This is otherwise known as continuous improvement. I believe the better our design, the fewer corrections we will need to fix the process.

I believe no one can get it right the first time every time. I think it is more rational, reasonable and realistic to focus on getting it right than being perfect — hence, the need for an eraser.

Life is a constant balancing act. The larger the correction, the more time, energy and money we will have to use to make things right or better.

Life is constantly changing. The sooner or further ahead we can anticipate and make corrections for improvement, the less effort we will need to perform the changes.

If we don't use an eraser to change, improve and adapt, we'll be like a dinosaur. Get left behind. Become obsolete. Eventually become extinct.

Now that we have gotten the more obvious ERASER discussions out of the way, I'd like to share with you my constant struggle with the material in this chapter.

This is by far the most difficult chapter for me to write in any of my books. I struggled with it for a long time. Trying to grasp the material. Trying to get it clear in my head. Trying to explain it simply. Like trying to catch my breath, it always wants to slip away. Like a cloud it fills the skies, but I cannot grasp it. Like a shadow it casts an image but has no weight. Like a reflection, I can see it but it is really not there.

I have to let go to be able to embrace it.

What is this elusive thing I am trying to chase?

Is it a thing I can hold with my hand?

Is it a thought I can catch in my brain?

Is it a feeling I can embrace in my heart?

I can't. It's — being full of emptiness.

It is a never-ending and constant effort to purge, maintain and preserve a clear and empty mind. I have to work at it, but I cannot achieve it by merely working hard. I have to try to relax my mind, but I cannot let go of my brain and let it wander. It seems so simple to say and do, but it is not easy for me.

The way I think about emptiness is the same way I view a kitchen sink.

We can't fill the sink up if it is already full. We have to empty it first. A kitchen sink full of dirty dishes has used up all its usefulness. A clean and empty kitchen sink is ready to be used and is more useful.

We can think about our brain like a kitchen sink too. And dirty dishes are like unclean thoughts. We cannot entertain a new thought if our old ways of thinking have filled up our head. We have to let go of the old to make room for the new — like emptying out and cleaning the sink.

"Emptiness is a high state of readiness."
—William Teh

The shape of the sink also determines how useful it is. The same can be said of our brains. Our mindsets and values determine the shape of our thinking. When we have an empty mind, we can entertain new thoughts or observations. Our mindset shapes how we feel, view and make use of what we gather and take in.

Sometimes we may have to change the shape (mindset) and size (capacity) of our kitchen sink for it to be more useful.

I believe developing, maintaining and adding value to grow meaningful relationships is more sustainable than trying to be the smartest, hardest working and most knowledgeable person in the room. It takes a little wisdom to put things into a better perspective. The best definition of being wise and being smart that I have read is this:

> *"To acquire knowledge, one must study;
> but to acquire wisdom, one must observe."*
> *—Marilyn vos Savant*

Having a clear head, clean heart and open hand can help us be more *abundantly* empty.

Here are my three takeaways to being *abundantly* empty.

Be Detached

Detachment is probably the opposite of desire. When we are able to detach ourselves of our desires, emotions and especially prejudices, we should be able to make better choices for a greater good.

When we are mad, sad or feel bad, our feelings get in the way of our brain making better decisions. Also in the book *Three Feet From Gold* Greg Reid noted in an interview with Ron Glosser:

"Never make a decision in a valley."

It is probably more helpful to seek the help or counsel of a good friend who is emotionally detached from our situation to help get us out of the valley.

Letting Go

When we are able to let go, we can relieve ourselves of the unnecessary garbage, baggage and luggage that we carry around in our brains, heart and closets. Most of the stuff we carry around, keep or horde is actually of no use to anyone else except ourselves. What is a good way to tell if our stuff is treasure or trash? Some pretty good indicators are: can our stuff can be sold or even given away? What will happen to our stuff after we die? Will it be kept or dumped?

Part of correctly letting go is knowing what to keep and what to toss.

Forgiving

What is forgiving? Merriam-Webster says forgiving is to cease feeling resentment against an offender. Forgiving, as I understand it, is actually letting go of a bad feeling. (*See discussion of letting go in the earlier paragraph.*)

When it comes to relationships, being able to forgive is like emptying out and cleansing our heart, so that we can start again. Unlike love, there are no attachments associated with forgiveness.

I believe some people like me have a difficult time forgiving because we think forgiving also means not punishing the person that offended or harmed us. Here is how I think about forgiveness and punishment.

We can be forgiven and *be* punished or be forgiven and *not be* punished.

We can punish the act of stealing, but we still can forgive the child. But sometimes we also have to look a little deeper into the motives for the act. For instance, if a child stole money from a cash register to buy medicine for his sick and dying mother, the motive was noble but the act was not. How do you punish a noble motive?

In some instances forgiving may do more good to the forgiver than the forgiven.

Here is how I think about forgiveness.

If the person annoys you, forgiving him is like taking a pebble out of your shoe so that you can perform (walk or run) better.

If the person hurts you, forgiving him is like pulling a thorn out of your flesh so that you can get rid of the pain, heal, and move on.

If the person hurts (emotionally) and harms (physically) you, or worse yet, that person hurts or harms someone you love like your children if you have any, you may absolutely HATE him. If hating him totally consumes you and makes you feel *bitter*, resentful and angry, not forgiving him is like allowing him to poison your soul, freeze your heart, and mess with your brain.

If you are in a horrible situation of hating someone, think about forgiveness this way. Let's say I am stupid enough to go mountain climbing alone. An accident happened and I am stuck on a frozen mountaintop with my foot crushed and trapped under a rock.

Night is coming and the *bitter* temperatures will freeze me to death before I can see the light of day again. Forgiving may be like cutting off my trapped limb before night falls so that I can drag myself down the mountain to live another day.

Leaving your crushed limb behind for the better good of your whole body may be a better choice than letting it slowly and surely kill you.

A key takeaway is not to allow your stupidity (like climbing a mountain by yourself) to slowly and surely kill you.

In the end, we may never get everything right. Constantly emptying out the garbage in our brains and unnecessary stuff in our closets can help us get fewer things wrong. It can also be very liberating.

With less stuff to manage, there will also be fewer opportunities to make mistakes.

Forgiving is like erasing the feelings of bitterness, hurts and resentments. *Rubbing out* the bad feelings can help us breathe more freely, walk more lightly and live more gently.

For those of us who have been broken by disappointments, discouragement or despair, allow me to encourage you with a picture of these three pencils.

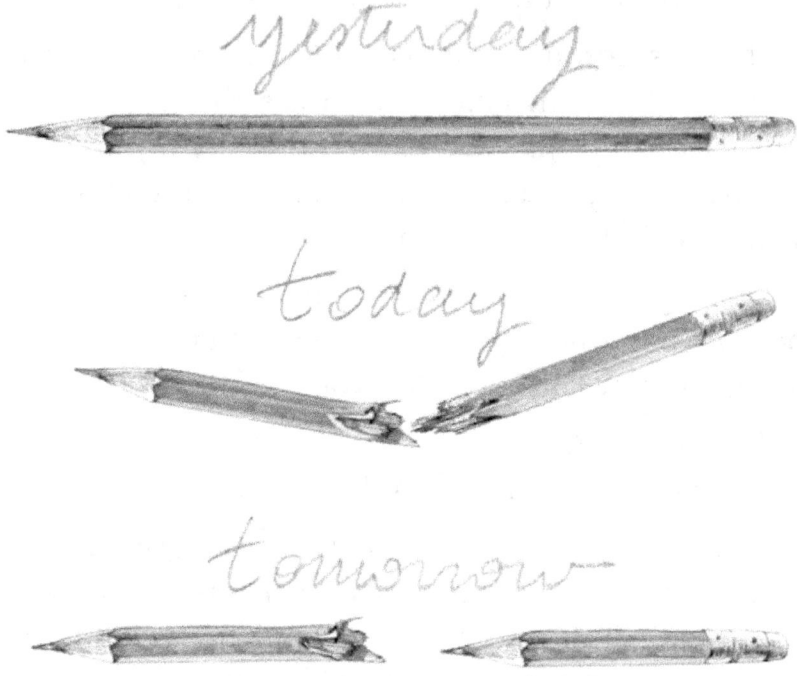

Chapter 14

The Last Chapter for a Good Friend

| **This space is intentionally left blank** | *"To the world you may be one person; but to one person you may be the world."* —Dr. Seuss |

This chapter is written with both sadness and relief to my dear friend Eugene (Gene) Vasconi. Gene passed away peacefully on July 20, 2018, after his battles with one type of cancer after another.

Gene frequently told amusing stories regarding his battle with cancer. Very few including myself understood and knew of the pain he endured. Gene even wrote a book called *For Bladder ... Or Worse*, a humorous story about his fight with bladder cancer.

The cancer spread from his bladder to his kidney to liver, and then it finally got the better of him. Gene always had a funny story or recap for me when he described his doctor and hospital visits. Gene is able to make up funny stories using the most unlikely, unusual and unpleasant situations to cheer up people around him.

I fondly address Gene as Dr. Vasconi. Why Dr. Vasconi? Because I came to first know Gene as the media doctor through an introduction made in 2011. Gene promoted himself as the media doctor because he could cure your media problems.

Since then we have eaten together, invested together, and thankfully managed to play a couple of rounds of golf together! By the way, Gene also helped me publish my first five books.

The three joys I enjoy with Gene are: friendship, humor and graciousness.

Friendship

I never knew how short a three-hour meal could be until I ate lunch with Gene. Generally it takes us about a half hour after we sit down before we even look at the menu, and I don't even know why. We go to the same restaurant. Come at the same time. Eat the same food.

After we talked to get our book and investment projects out of the way, Gene would say, "Let's get to the good stuff."

THE LAST CHAPTER FOR A GOOD FRIEND

One of our more recent "good stuff" conversations involved playing golf.

Gene played golf once or twice a year with his long-time musician friend. I play golf once or twice every other year. There are golfers and there are landscapers. I belong to the latter. We were fairly evenly matched, or rather . . . equally bad.

We talked at length about how poorly we each played golf but had not experienced each other's inability to hit a ball or ability to move a pile of dirt with a stick. Finally, in 2017, we made a devious plan to actually go chase a ball around.

There are only three decent months in a year to play golf in Central Texas according to Gene. The other nine months are plagued with unbearable summer heat, terrible allergies, and bugs the size of humming birds. This was Gene's story, and I bought into it.

At an aggressive rate of playing one game a month for three months a year, I calculated that it would take us 10 years to play 30 rounds of golf. If Gene had beaten cancer, it would have put him at age 80 and me over 60. I'd say that sounds about the right pace.

Gene was already huffing and puffing, thinking about the last couple of years to knock out the last half-dozen games of golf when I shared with him my pro forma analysis. Ha! I was able to make the good doctor sweat — and not over the hot cup of tea he was drinking.

With one set of clubs divided into two bags, we tackled the golf course. Gene took the even-numbered clubs, and I took the odd-numbered sticks. Why? Because he couldn't swing the odd numbered sticks, and I don't know how to use even-numbered clubs — and neither one of us knows what a driver is used for besides losing golf balls.

I am glad we got to play two out of our 30 planned games of golf.

If you want to do something important, put it on your schedule and do it now. Every opportunity we throw away is an opportunity we waste. I would have deeply regretted if Gene and I talked about playing golf together but never actually played.

Humor

Gene is a master at weaving mundane stories into tales that can turn laughter into tears. How he passed on investing in a house because it was so close to the airport the low flying taking off or landing planes would rattle the fillings in his mouth every half hour. How he used dog treats to tame a 300-pound wild salivating beast from eating him—his neighbor's 12-year-old German Shepherd.

Even after hanging out with Gene for over half a dozen years, I am *still* a student at trying to use humor to start, build and deepen relationships. I used to be terrible. Now I am just bad.

Graciousness

Earlier this year before Gene was hospitalized, I shared with him a rough draft of the book you are holding in your hand. Gene read it for entertainment value, content

THE LAST CHAPTER FOR A GOOD FRIEND

and usefulness. He thought the material was pretty good, but I will leave the final verdict up to you.

I would have loved to have Gene help me again as he did with my previous books. That would have created another reason for us to eat lunch together. Instead, he suggested I consider getting a second opinion or another set of eyes to review my manuscript. I was not keen on the idea, but the more I thought about it, it dawned on me to use his suggestion to take our relationship to the next level. We could free up more time to talk and do more of the *good stuff.*

Gene was preparing to wind down his businesses, especially with his constant and never-ending battles with cancer so that he could spend more time with his family and do more of the things he loved but had been putting off.

That was why Gene recommended that I connect with Mel of Inspired Authors Press, the editor and publishing consultant for this book.

Gene reviewed my draft at his desk in his home office and again in bed at the hospital. Even while in the hospital, Gene offered to edit and publish "Paper Pencil Eraser" for me if I chose not to use Mel. I urged him to focus on getting more rest. Reading my drafts at night would only want to make him jump out of bed at 1:26am, drive across town at 67 miles per hour in his hospital gown to bang on my door and pour a bucket of ice water on my head. He'd want to scream at me and tell me it would take a mountain of time and work just to make my book even barely readable. But that would at least get the good doctor out of bed. By the way, I have never heard Dr. Vasconi talk loud enough for me to hear him from more than three feet away.

Dr. Vasconi, not only did you hold my hand for more than six years, you helped me edit and publish my first five books. You were always so gracious doing what you thought was better for me. You put my interests above your own. Without my knowing (and maybe you too), you were preparing to pass the baton over to Mel to continue to help me publish my books. Mel is equally as gracious to pick up the baton to take care of me so that I don't stall, fumble or get off track.

Mel is now holding my hand so we can publish *Paper Pencil Eraser*. Mel is like you; he is pretty tough on me too. Ugh! He gives me homework, assignments and corrections to do, just like you did. Actually, even more! Mel, I appreciate you for helping me polish, button up and share "Paper Pencil Eraser" with the world.

At our last meal together, one of the "good stuff" conversations we talked about was living our lives backwards. Of course we went to the same restaurant. Came at the same time. And ate the same food. Duh!

I asked Gene what he would like to have written for his eulogy. Gene was humored by my question and asked me to clarify what I meant. "Well," I said, "It's like I always try to begin with the end in mind first with all my projects. I try to back out what I want to accomplish before I even begin to think about doing it. It's a lot of work preparing, doing and repairing anything worthwhile. It is the same for my life."

Therefore, if I already know what I want to be remembered for, I can start living my life like the way I want be remembered; then whomever draws the short straw to write my eulogy will have a much easier time doing so.

As we continued to explore the topic, I asked Gene what he would like to have written on his headstone. He thought for a while and said that it was difficult to come up with one thing that he liked. Upon deeper reflection, Gene said that if he could pick only one thing, it would be this, "He was a good husband." Why did Gene choose to be finally remembered as a good husband? Well, he was married to his wife and life partner Pam for 29 years and they did not have children. He thought the world of Pam.

> *"To the world you may be one person;*
> *but to one person you may be the world."*
> —Dr. Seuss

Dr. Vasconi, I am blessed to be able the share a meal, chase a golf ball, and sit for a while together with you. Sharing these times with you has enriched my life. You poured yourself into me and helped water the seeds of friendship, humor and graciousness.

I am grateful to you for your guidance, friendship and companionship.

Dr. Vasconi, you are a good friend, and I will always remember you fondly. I miss you.

Chapter 15

Composing Your Story

"In the end, only three things matter: how much you loved, how gently you lived, and how gracefully you let go of the things not meant for you."
—Buddha

Now that we have a better understanding of the power of a piece of paper, a pencil, and an eraser, we can use them to compose a nice story of our lives.

The only one stopping you now is YOU. Don't let anyone tell you otherwise. We can compose a storybook life for ourselves because we can doodle the pictures, write the songs, and make up the stories.

> *"Be the author to the story of your life."*
> —William Teh

Remember, if you need help with writing a better story for your life, you can find and get help from someone who is living or has lived a better storybook life. No one says you have to write your story by yourself.

Another way I have heard or read it is this way: When you are a servant to your purpose, you will not have to be a slave to the urgent.

> *"When you become a servant to your purpose, you will not have to be a slave to the urgent."*

There is one special charm that you NEED to make your story come alive. *You have to write or at least be involved in writing your story.* Happiness, like abundance, if handed to you will not work. You have to labor for it. Two-thirds of making your story come alive is for you to write it, and the other one-third is purposefully living it.

Don't write your story one way and live your life another way. You don't have to get your story perfect; you just have to get it right.

The magic of your story is not so much WHAT you get out of it but rather WHO you become. WHO is the character you want to become as a result of your story? You get to decide. You get to pick your character. You get to play the character. You are the storywriter.

A good story we write will play out well when we enjoy and are qualified to play the character we choose. The story will not unfold well when we try to play a role that we are not suited to play.

To better enjoy our story together with the other characters in our storybook, remind:

Our Head

How *PREPARED* we end the day determines how *READY* we start tomorrow.

Our Head and Hands

How *RESTED* we end the day determines how *WELL* we start tomorrow.

Our Head, Hands and Heart

How *WELL* we have lived, loved and laughed determines how gracefully we *LET GO* or *let a loved one go* when we go.

Keeping things simple is not easy. Maybe that's why so few people can do it. Like water, life is better when it is pure.

> *"Like water, life is better when it is pure."*
> —William Teh

Allow me to conclude this chapter and book with a vacation story.

In June of 2018, I took my family on a vacation trip to Costa Rica. Costa Rica is well known for being one of the happiest countries in the world. The only thing more lovely than the country are its people. Costa Ricans are welcoming, warm and friendly.

One of the phrases I commonly heard in Costa Rica was, "Pura Vida" which means *simple life* or *pure life*. In Costa Rica it is more than just a greeting; it is a way of life.

I met some of the most cheerful and lovely people in Costa Rica. Our driver, Fernando, took us from the San Jose Airport to Mount Arenal. He and his wife are expecting their first baby boy in 7 months. Fernando explained to us that he is putting in more driving time so that when his wife delivers, he will have a little more money in his pocket and can take more days off to spend time with his wife and new baby.

After three fantastic days in Mount Arenal, another driver named Junior drove us to Playa Conchal (shell beach) to spend our last four days in Costa Rica.

I tend to wake up early even on vacation, so that I can have a little time to myself and drink my cup of coffee before everyone wakes up. This morning I was faced with a challenge after finishing breakfast.

I have three items I like to take to the beach with me: 1) my book; 2) my coffee; and 3) my smoothie. However, with only two hands, I can only carry two of the three things. I texted Gene to ask how he thought I would decide. Yes, Gene was correct. I took the book and the coffee.

First I chugged down the untasty but healthy smoothie and then carried my book and coffee down to the beach. There and then I settled down to enjoy my book, sip my coffee, and drink in the view.

My takeaway: As Brian Tracy says, "Eat your frog first." (Do your most important thing first.)

Later, after everybody woke up and ate breakfast, we went down to the beach again to check out the sand, water and waves. Nathan and I jumped into the ocean, while Hannah and Mama (not comfortable with the surf) washed their feet in the water.

I told Nathan to watch for big waves coming and to jump up as they hit us. If we caught the wave correctly, we could bob up and down like a cork when the wave picked us up. It was fun for a couple of boys from central Texas.

Regrouping on the beach, I asked what everyone would like to do next. Mama thought she'd like to try a beach massage to iron out the kinks in her back, and Hannah wanted to read her book with Mama. Nathan looked out at the invitingly warm ocean and *decided* that he would like to go kayaking.

"Nice plans," I thought. "Nathan, would you like to check out the kayaks for rent?" I asked. "No. I'd rather stay here with Mama," he replied because that sounded like work. "OK," I said. And I began to walk back up the beach to the equipment rental station.

There I met a wonderful young man named Jesus who helped check out a couple of sea kayaks. After completing some paperwork, with a big-hearted smile, he picked up two kayaks, dragged them down to the water, and helped launch Nathan and I into the ocean.

Jesus explained the do's and don'ts of how to paddle safely. He also pointed to a big rock-like island in what looked like the middle of the ocean. He told us that is as far out as we should go, and that if we ran into trouble, we'd still be in sight and he'd come get us. No problem, I thought. I wouldn't go farther out than I can stand and pee in the ocean if it were up to me. Then he pushed us off.

We had a great time. We paddled. We raced. We drifted. I especially enjoyed sitting and drifting in the ocean as Nathan and I had a nice father and son chat. We talked about the vacation. We talked about school. We talked about boy stuff. We enjoyed floating quietly in the middle of the sea.

Eventually, it was time to go back. Jesus met us on the beach and asked if we had a good time. "Pura Vida!" I answered. Jesus then dragged both kayaks back up the beach out of reach of the high tide.

Wearing nothing but a pair of swim shorts and a rubber hotel ID wristband, I could only offer him a grateful smile for his help. But I did give him a nice tip the next day.

Nathan and I walked up the beach behind Jesus. "Nathan, can I ask you a question?" "What is it Papa?" Nathan replied.

"Five frogs are sitting on a log. One decides to jump off. How many frogs are on the log?" Nathan had heard me ask this question before and lowered his eyes. He knew where I was going. "Papa, is this another business lesson?" "Yes," I said.

"Five, Papa," Nathan said softly. "Five frogs." I continued, "So even though you decided to go kayaking, you chose to stay and enjoy the beach with Mama while I went to pick up the kayaks. Would we have gone kayaking if I did not take action?" "No Papa, I understand," Nathan said. "OK. Remember that next time. Now let's go look for Mama and Hannah, get something to eat and drink, and jump into the swimming pool."

My takeaway: *Nothing good happens without taking the right action, even when a good thing is in front of us.*

If you are not living the life you want, and have not composed a storybook life for your life, do it now. Your story will not write itself. Remember, you can always pull out your eraser to rub out parts you don't like and make things better. It does not have to be perfect; it just has to be right. But remember there is nothing to erase if you only have a blank sheet of paper.

As you begin to put down this book, I'd like to thank you for sharing this time together with me. If you have found value in these pages, consider multiplying the value you have received by giving away some Paper, Pencils and Erasers (or more simply, this book) to your friends and family.

One day when I close the last page in my book of life, I want you—Mama Teh, Koko Teh, and Ah Ling—to know that you are the most beautiful chapters of my life.

Pura Vida

OTHER BOOKS BY WILLIAM TEH

This book is a collection of 13 chapters of simple strategies that I discovered as I labored to pursue a more abundant life for my family and me. I realized that freedom of choice, free time, and my health are my most important assets.

¡Wow! Este libro está lleno de conocimiento, contenido y una cantidad de sabiduría asombrosa. William ha escrito un libro brillante, discutiendo 13 estrategias que usa para crear más tiempo libre y producir dinero sin mucho esfuerzo. Utilizando sus ideas usted puede vivir una vida más satisfactoria. William comparte sus historias con usted como si estuvieran tomando el té. El libro estáescrito de una manera sencilla y puede ser leído sin mucho esfuerzo.

William Teh's second offering that explores how readers can become happier. A collection of a dozen simple and overlooked concepts hidden (as he says) in broad daylight. This small book packs in some amazing concepts that are easy to make a part of your life and will make a huge difference. This book will change your life!

William Teh's third book in his series about living life better. An easy to read, colorful keepsake that you will be proud and excited to recommend to others. William's simple style will have you on the road to a more simple and relationship-rich lifestyle in no time.

OTHER BOOKS BY WILLIAM TEH

This easy to read book is packed with insight and inspirational stories that can be easily applied to one's financial and personal life. William has brought to the forefront wisdom and logic that has faded from modern everyday life. The lessons on how to identify, understand and prioritize what is important to the individual can help in creating plans to grow wealth in all aspects of life.

I wrote this book not because I am qualified to write about this topic but because I wished I could have read a book like this when I was younger and had less ZEST for life. Now I am getting a little older, a little greyer, and a lot slower. Traveling on this path I call 'my life', I appreciate the shoulders to lean on when I am weary, and cheer me on when I feel like giving up.

www.ingramcontent.com/pod-product-compliance
Lightning Source LLC
Chambersburg PA
CBHW071927290426
44110CB00013B/1510